EMPEROR FRANZ JOSEPH
1830–1916
Myth and Truth

Katrin Unterreiner

EMPEROR FRANZ JOSEPH
1830–1916
Myth and Truth

Translated by Martin Kelsey

CHRISTIAN BRANDSTÄTTER VERLAG
WIEN

TABLE OF CONTENTS

PREFACE

Emperor Franz Joseph ruled over the Austrian monarchy for sixty-eight years, leaving a lasting mark on the history of Europe. He nevertheless failed to distinguish himself as one of the most politically significant monarchs, his reign instead being characterised by adherence to tradition, conservatism and fulfilment of bureaucratic duty. The intention of this book, however, is to present Franz Joseph much more as a private individual, rather than throwing the spotlight on the Emperor and his historical significance. The principle focus of interest here is his childhood. What was it like for little »Franzi« growing up at the court in Vienna, and what influence did his ambitious mother Archduchess Sophie have? Franz turns out to have been a surprisingly humorous and imaginative child, although he was later drilled to perform the role of dutiful Emperor. State business always came first, and was something to which he was prepared to sacrifice his private life. His wife Elisabeth whom he loved unconditionally throughout his life and with whom he enjoyed much greater matrimonial harmony than is often portrayed after enabling her to pursue her private life away from the Viennese court. Relations with his children were distant, his relationship with his only son being especially strained. However estranged Franz Joseph may have been from his children, he was, nevertheless, touching in his role as a grandfather. His grandchildren were not in the least in awe of him, the fact that he did not keep them at a distance himself enabling him to enjoy something approaching a family life in his final years. The main focus of the book, however, is the Emperor's everyday life. His valet Eugen Ketterl is the main conduit providing us with an opportunity to get to know the old Emperor at first hand and discover his sense of humour.

Opposite page:
Emperor Franz Joseph I. Painting by Wilhelm List from the conference room of the headquarters of the Austrian Post Savings Bank, constructed 1904-06 by Otto Wagner, around 1905.

Below:
Field marshal Emperor Franz Joseph. Colour Lithograph by Anton Strassgschwandtner, around 1870.

F.G.Waldmüller: Kaiser Franz Joseph I. als Kind.

Imperial Childhood

On 18 August 1830,
a small boy was born in
Schönbrunn Palace and
christened Franz Joseph
Karl. His parents Arch-
duke Franz Carl and
Archduchess Sophie were
beside themselves with
joy. After suffering a series
of miscarriages, Sophie
had fulfilled her para-
mount duty by providing
the dynasty with a
healthy son.

Above:
Archduchess Sophie
with the little Archduke
Franz, painting by Josef
Stieler, 1832.

Opposite page:
Franz at the age of three.
Photoengraving from
a painting by
Ferdinand Georg
Waldmüller, around 1833.

Archduchess Sophie.
Painting by Johann
Nepomuk Ender nach
Josef Carl Stieler,
around 1830.

TU FELIX AUSTRIA NUBE ...

Franz Joseph's mother was a remarkable woman. The daughter of the King of Bavaria Maximilian Joseph I, she was confident, strong-minded, had a keen mind, was educated and, above all, ambitious. All her sisters had made splendid matches and were Queens of Saxony and Prussia, her stepsister Karolina Augusta even having become Empress of Austria by dint of becoming the fourth wife of Emperor Franz I. The former had also immediately thought of her younger stepsister when the time came for the second son of the Emperor, Archduke Franz Karl, to marry. Marriages were a political business. For evidence of this, one need look no further than the famous dictum on the Habsburgs' marriage policy *Bella gerant alii – tu felix Austria nube* – »Others may wage war. You, oh happy Austria, marry«. This motto applied to all the dynasties. Daughters were political footballs, were raised in line with this philosophy and mostly concurred with parental decisions without offering any resistance. The paramount principle was to continue the dynasty, or as State Chancellor Metternich put it: The reason we get married is to have children, not to fulfil our hearts' desires.

Although Archduke Franz Karl did not suffer from serious illness like his older brother Crown Prince Ferdinand, he had little in the way of intellectual talent and was certainly far from being an equal partner for Sophie. The couple's first meeting came as a shock for her, and she wrote to her mother: *He is a bon garcon, he asks everyone's advice, mais il est terrible ... he would bore me to death!* Despite all this, the heir to the throne was ill and not predicted to live long. This meant that Sophie would have a realistic chance of becoming Empress herself, were she to enter into this marriage. The marriage between the disparate couple took place in 1824 and, when Sophie finally fulfilled her duty six years later by giving birth to a son, she was in a position not only to consolidate her position at court but to make clever use of it to further her own interests. In stark contrast to her husband, the Archduchess was interested in politics and, within a short space of time, was able to establish important allies and confidants. The fact that the court, and Emperor Franz in particular, were completely smitten with little Franzi led her to form the aim she now relentlessly pursued: her son should be Emperor one day.

THE IMPERIAL NURSERY

Archduke Franz Karl.
Photograph by
Rosa Jenik, 1872.

Louise Baroness Sturmfeder was appointed »Aja«, or governess of little Franzi, as he was lovingly named within the family. She loved the little boy as if her were her own child, her affectionate yet strict upbringing leaving its mark on him in later life. Baroness Sturmfeder loved order, was religious and held the firm conviction that spoiled and pampered children grew up to be effete and weak adults. This also applied to physical inurement. Baroness Sturmfeder was not a woman who was lacking in confidence, even daring to act against the recommendations or even the instructions issued by the court doctor Dr. Malfatti. Her view was that Franzi should not spend the whole of the winter in his room as usual. Even ventilation was generally looked upon with disdain at the time, since fresh air was thought to contain *poisonous miasma*. The whole court was in uproar when it became known that she had been out

Archduke Franz as a small child, lithograph by Dauthage, around 1831.

for a walk with the little archduke in bad weather. To general surprise, the small boy grew into a robust child rather than being constantly ill. Things came to a head between Sturmfeder and Malfatti just after one Christmas, when Franz's presents had included a tambourine. Malfatti wanted to take the toy away from the child, fearing that, since it was not padded, he might injure himself. Baroness Sturmfeder, concerned to provide the imperial children with as normal an upbringing as possible, at least in their early years, protested vehemently, informed Archduchess Sophie, expressing the view that Malfatti was going too far, since otherwise *the child would have to be brought up in a padded box*. Sophie agreed with her.

Louise Baroness Sturmfeder, the Aja of the Archduke. Photograph, around 1870.

THE MAGIC OF UNIFORM

As early as the age of ten months, little Franzi was already displaying his fascination for all things military. He hardly ever missed the drama of the changing of the guard in the Innerer Burghof which saw the new guard marching in complete with drums and trumpets. Sophie had a small uniform made for him and gave him a small wooden rifle, with which he was constantly to be seen presenting arms. She expressed her delight in a letter to her mother: *You wouldn't believe how prettily he can do that. He is absolutely adorable with his little rifle, his infantryman's cap on his head, his sabre at his side and the small knapsack on his back. When I arrived home latterly, he was waiting in front of my door, ready to present arms as I entered ...* At eighteen months old, he could

The Swiss part at the Hofburg Palace: Swiss Gate (1552), splendid Renaissance gate in the oldest part of the palace. Photograph by Wilfried Vas.

Franzi spent his childhood at the Hofburg Palace in Vienna and at Schönbrunn Palace, with some stays in Ischl. Especially the Hofburg was the very opposite of a splendid and luxurious residence. Many of the enormous rooms had makeshift glass walls to create space and to allow for better heating. But this was not all. The windows of the apartment in the Treasury, occupied by Franz Joseph, were directly above the »privy« used by the guards posted directly beneath him, making the smells virtually unbearable, especially in summer.

differentiate between the *Azizis* (officers) and the *Dada* (men), his greatest pleasure being watching the soldiers drill. When he was twenty months old, he was practising marching lockstep with his father and grandfather, calling out orders such a *Halt* and *Quick March*, although he had trouble pronouncing the latter. By the time he was three years old, he knew about all the army's honours and the colours of the individual regiments.

Archduke Franz offers a gift to a sentry. Painting by Peter Fendi, 1836.

Franzi was allowed to undertake regular walks with his Imperial grandfather, and Peter Fendl captures one event (from 1833) in this picture. Out walking in the Laxenburg Palace Park, the Emperor, his wife and Franzi came across a sentry, and the small Archduke expressed a wish to make the soldier a present of a banknote. The sentry presenting arms, however, was not permitted to move. The Emperor then said to his grandson: *Go up to him Franzi, and put the money in his cartridge bag. That's not against orders. He's not allowed to take it in his hand.*

LITTLE FRANZI

The marriage of Crown Prince Ferdinand to Maria Anna of Savoy shortly after the birth of his nephew Franz Joseph weakened Sophie's position at court, and she now began to make clever use of her major asset, her delightful young son. There were numerous portraits of the adorable little archduke, and Sophie made a particularly conscious effort to establish his popularity with the general populace as well as at court. To show off her son to the enthusiastic Viennese, she often took him for a walk in Schönbrunn Park, also giving audiences with the child on her arm. Every day after dinner, Sophie brought little Franzi to the Emperor in his study, where the two played together for an hour, the Emperor becoming the small boy's idol. The attraction was mutual, Franzi, a pretty and good-tempered child, gradually becoming the Emperor's favourite grandchild.

Another of his very favourite playmates at the time was his cousin, the Duke of Reichstadt. When Sophie had arrived at the Viennese Court at the age of nineteen, the grandson of Emperor Franz I, son of Archduchess Marie Luise and Napoleon, was just thirteen years old. The young duke was an admirer of his beautiful aunt and, although the later was initially amused by his sentimentality, a friendship gradually formed between the two which, in turn, led to the Duke of Reichstadt's spending a considerable amount of time with little Franzi.

No confirmation can be found regarding any relationship between Sophie and the young duke. Also given the watchful eyes of the Viennese court and the fact that he was six years younger, it is scarcely credible that the ambitious but also deeply religious Sophie was bound to her nephew by more than friendship, although her unprepossessing husband made her wish to spend time with the attractive and charming duke understandable.

In 1835, when Franz Joseph was just five years old, Emperor Franz I died and his son Ferdinand became Emperor.

Above:
Emperor Franz I in the ceremonial robes of the Order of the Golden Fleece. Painting by Friedrich Amerling, 1832.

Left:
Emperor Ferdinand I. Painting by Leopold Kupelwieser, 1847.

»The little deity«

Emperor Ferdinand was ill and infertile and, it being readily apparent after a period of time that no progeny were to be expected, Archduchess Sophie began a deliberate policy of bringing up her son Franzi as a future Emperor of Austria. The cheerful little boy was gradually moulded into the perfect heir to the throne, a process which involved the Archduke »enjoying« an extremely strict upbringing from his earliest childhood, something which was to leave its mark on him in later life. Sophie educated him according to her absolute conviction of the rule of God's grace rather than impressing on him any unshakeable feeling of being something special. She began a conscious policy of isolating her son as a way of underlining his particular status at court. Sophie also closely monitored his environment and the people having contact with her son, only very few children fulfilling the criteria required to be the playmates of a future emperor. Although Sophie was an

Emperor Franz with his grandchildren in his study. Watercolour by Peter Fendi, 1834.

ambitious mother, relentlessly pursuing her aim of making her son Emperor, she was, at the same time, a caring and proud parent. Her *Le petit chou*, her pet name for her son, was her whole world. In May 1831, she wrote to her mother: *You cannot imagine how excellently this dear little boy is developing, or of how pretty, lively, intelligent, good and tender he is ...* Whenever he was ill, she cared for him devotedly, never leaving his side for a second. She went to such extremes that the court even dubbed him the *little deity*. Sophie enjoyed the major advantage of not being Empress, her position as archduchess leaving her free to concentrate on her role as a mother. She was later to expect very different priorities from her daughter-in-law Empress Elisabeth, requiring the fulfilment of her duties as Empress alongside Franz Joseph.

At the age of two, Franzi carried out his first »representative« duty during the Corpus Christi procession, a major event for the strictly Catholic Habsburg Monarchy and a source of the greatest pride to his mother. When he was four, he made his first appear-

Family reunion of the Austrian Imperial household in autumn 1834. Watercolour by Peter Fendi.

ance at a court banquet, and his military training began after the Christmas celebrations of 1834.

Franzi's daily routine was now planned down to the tiniest detail. He rose at seven, his lessons beginning half an hour later and continuing, apart from some short breaks, until seven in the evening. This was followed by dinner and bed at eight in the evening.

»Joining the Men«

The next break took place when he reached his seventh birthday. Until this point, Franz had grown up in the so-called nursery, together with his brothers Ferdinand Max, born in 1832 and Carl Ludwig, born in 1833, being in the tender care of his *Amie*, as he lovingly called Baroness Sturmfeder, for his education. Now, however, he moved into his own apartment and, in line with tradition, »joined the men«. It broke Baroness Sturmfeder's heart to have to give up her little Franzi and henceforth also to be permitted no contact with him. Although she remained the Aja of his younger brothers for the time being, they also ultimately grew out of the nursery and she received a small flat in the Hofburg, from

Emperor Franz Joseph's child's uniform. Tunic of the Infantry Regiment No. 4 with matching pantaloons and helmet.

where she was mostly only able to observe »her children« from a distance. Tradition has it that the only contact she had with the boys, who for their part also missed her painfully from within their new »man's household« consisted in her children's lowering secret messages and presents to her attached to a piece of twine from where they lived directly above her, and Baroness Sturmfeder responding in the same fashion with small pictures and letters.

When it came to the selection of a new tutor for the archduke, the responsibility of the function he was to fulfil duly according him an important status at court, political reasons naturally outweighed any educational considerations. The choice was made by State Chancellor Metternich, who gave the following simple reason for deciding on Heinrich Count Bombelles: *I class Bombelles as belonging to the small group of people who possess the congenital inclination to think as I would think, see things as they are and to want the same as I would want.* Although Sophie was far from happy, Bombelles being the son of a virtually impoverished French diplomat, the fact that he was a devout Catholic finally won her over. Sophie knew full well that the position of »Primo Ajo« was more in the nature of an overall custodian and that, in reality, the steward was the tutor and usually wielded far more in the way of influence. She held the latter position and appointed Colonel Johann Alexander Count of Coronini-Cronberg, a soldier of the old school, strict, stiff and pedantic and offering rigid military discipline as a counterweight to his lack of imagination. He now took on the task of making a soldier out of the cheerful little Franzi.

Archduchess Sophie continued to take her role as the mother of a future Emperor very seriously. She took part in lessons and

A puzzle of »The coats of arms of the major European states«, around 1830, a possession from the Imperial household (handed down through the Habsburg-Este line, Dukes of Modena)

This Imperial toy provides evidence of the dual function of such playthings, which always had an associated pedagogical aspect rather than being intended »merely« as a toy. Toys were considered as part of the preparations for adulthood and served an educational purpose as well as providing entertainment. It was no coincidence that the young Archdukes played with military toys. These actually represented reality in a miniature form rather than constituting any kind of plaything. The medium of play was in effect a way of introducing the children to their adult roles and equipping them for later life.

Steam operated locomotive belonging to Archduke Franz.

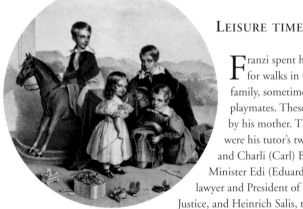

monitored the teachers, as well as checking the staff and their housekeeping in her son's apartment. She took the Archduke to official events, especially military parades, proudly reporting how delighted her Franzi had been with the cannon and rifle fire in his immediate proximity which had taken place on the occasion of a state visit.

Franz's delight was genuine. Since his infancy, his preference for military matters had not only remained, but had intensified. He loved military parades and, whereas his brother Max was visibly bored by the marches, Franzi was full of enthusiasm, announcing afterwards that he had never seen anything more beautiful in his whole life.

From the age of eight onwards, Franz's lesson time was increased to thirty-seven hours a week, and he proved to be a dutiful, obedient and conscientious pupil from the very start. Coronini's strict educational methods brought out in him a marked predilection for orderly work and bureaucratic tasks, something described by the former tutor of Emperor Franz I Count Colloredo, however, as *a preference for inanities*. The main thing learned by Franzi, who had been spending virtually the whole of the day at his desk since the age of five, was that punctual fulfilment of his duty was more important than content, his own thoughts and views quickly being banished from his mind.

Franz with his brothers Ferdinand Maximilian and Carl Ludwig and his sister Anna, who died at the age of four. Lithograph, around 1835.

LEISURE TIME

Franzi spent his brief leisure time going for walks in the Prater and visiting family, sometimes being allowed to invite playmates. These, of course, were selected by his mother. The most frequent visitors were his tutor's two sons Marko (Markus) and Charli (Carl) Bombelles, the future Prime Minister Edi (Eduard) Taaffe, son of the court lawyer and President of the Supreme Office of Justice, and Heinrich Salis, the son of the High Court

Master of Archduke Franz Karl. He spent most of the time with his brothers, however, in summer mostly in the Schönbrunn Palace Park which afforded the dukes the necessary space and opportunity to play. The boys were particularly fond of playing in a separately laid out garden in the Meidlinger Hollow, the so-called Bowling Green, where they had been provided with an area for playing, gymnastics and drill. There was also a Red Indian hut for Max, who had been fascinated by foreign countries since he had been a small child, a range of gymnastic equipment, a swing and a rabbit hutch. Other animals which the children had been given as pres-

ents, such as sheep and goats, were also kept here. Max, for example, who loved animals above all else, had received in 1839 a special present for his seventh birthday: *a volière with 24 birds, a parrot, a small deer, a guinea pig, two squirrels, in short a complete menagerie, which is exactly what he had requested. A small garden with an absolutely delicious Red Indian hut had been set up for him, all sorts of Red Indian equipment, a hammock slung between two trees, all surrounded by an array of the loveliest flowers and plants, pineapples having been planted in the earth.* The children were less enthused by the swimming lessons which took place in the pond behind the obelisk fountain. The water was ice cold, but whereas Max and Carl Ludwig protested every time they had to go into the water, Franzi managed to maintain his composure and was well behaved, performing his exercises as ordered without offering any resistance.

Sophie was thrilled and pleased that Franzi, in contrast to his brothers, did not cause any trouble. Compared to his older brother, Max had poorer powers of concentration and was more exuberant and more rumbustious. Sophie was ill at ease with the childish nature of her second son, writing to her mother: *Maxi is very lazy*

Franz, Ferdinand Max and Carl Ludwig on the Boulengreen in Schönbrunn Park. Watercolour by Franz Barbarini, around 1839/40.

The Boulengreen is a sandy square used for playing boules or boccia. The Imperial children also used this part of the Palace Park as a playground. In the watercolour, the children can be seen playing with a miniature fire engine. Carl Ludwig is stroking a deer.

and too much of a chatterbox, because his lively imagination always gets the better of him. Although he is frequently berated, this is like speaking to a cow. Most of Sophie's concerns, however, were reserved for her third son, Carl Ludwig: *He comes across as a small, fat farmer's boy and when the court priest summons up all his patience and believes he has made him comprehend something, he only needs to utter a single word to make it plain that he has understood nothing at all.*

»THE IMPORTANCE OF SPECTACLE«

The Habsburgs had developed a particular enthusiasm for theatrical performances as early as the 17th century, taking part in the performances themselves as actors, dancers and singers. This meant that participation in theatre, opera and ballet performances had established itself as an integral part of the education and everyday life of the Imperial children. Especially since the time of Maria Theresia, theatre performances had been a regular element of activities within the family circle, and nothing had changed. Sophie also maintained the tradition and had the children rehearse theatre performances, although these were by no means limited to family entertainment in the evenings. The Habsburgs had always seen a connection between theatre and educational purpose. The idea behind these small performances was for the children to build up confidence and for them to allay their shyness in addressing large numbers of people. Franz always knew his lines off by heart, although his delivery did not contain much in the way of emotion. Max, on the other hand, declaimed his part with great commitment and pathos, was, however, regularly susceptible to mental blocks. Baroness Sturmfeder described a similar situation in a letter to her family: *I spent the evening with the children … Franzi read poems out loud. His memory is remarkable. He reads the poem and is then immediately able to repeat a few stanzas to you by heart. Today, he told me he prefers Schiller to Goethe. Quite a statement from a child who is only ten years old. Ferdinand Max listens attentively, refused to put up with some of it, since he says it makes him have nightmares. Carl did not take much part in proceedings …*

Max, not expecting to succeed to the throne at that time, was able to enjoy an untroubled childhood, and his development continued along these lines. Franz had already been turned into a dutiful and precocious Emperor wide beyond his years.

»The Muddle by Kotzebue in five acts« – programme for a performance by Archduke Franz and Archduke Ferdinand Max.

Childhood letters

Whenever the young archduke received a rare opportunity to escape drill, a quite different set of characteristics came to the fore. Franz's childhood letters show him displaying a considerable level of imagination and humour, the accompanying caricatures and remarks even revealing an element of disrespect, quite different to other biographies, which always portray him as serious, conscientious and, above all, unimaginative. These letters, written by Franz to his brother when one of them was ill, thus bringing about their separation, make it clear that not even the well-behaved archduke was free from moods where he succumbed to the arrogance of youth. For a play he was staging, for example, he secretly planned to incorporate a fire to be followed by a flood, as well as devising other »spectacles«:

Dear Maxi!
Forgive me, forgive me! Time is short. Learning in the mornings, and grandmother comes in the evening, so the day passes; but tomorrow, dear Monsieur, I hope that Mr Grosselet will be up on his horse, I have already started working on him, but to day I have started to put together the little play in which I intend to play Karlen; I also plan to have a fire which will be started by spirit, a flood and many other spectacles. This morning, we were with grandmother where a mass was read for grandfather, today being the 12th of February.
Farewell, Your Excellency. Your Excellency's most devoted servant
Franz Joseph
I beg you to tell Count Bomb.(elles) *that the counts and the teachers* (accompanied by a caricature)

Yesterday, we saw Talbot who looked as follows
(Caricature with the following remarks numbered)
1 half torn hat, perhaps 10 years old
2 badly arranged curls half hanging into her face
3 very blotchy boa
4 Terrible old dress

Best wishes to Wittek (the young archdukes' teacher of Czech and calligraphy)

Mr Doré (the archdukes' French teacher) *very much regrets that you are ill and is delighted to hear you are feeling better. Mr Hoffer wishes the same.*
Now it is finally finished.

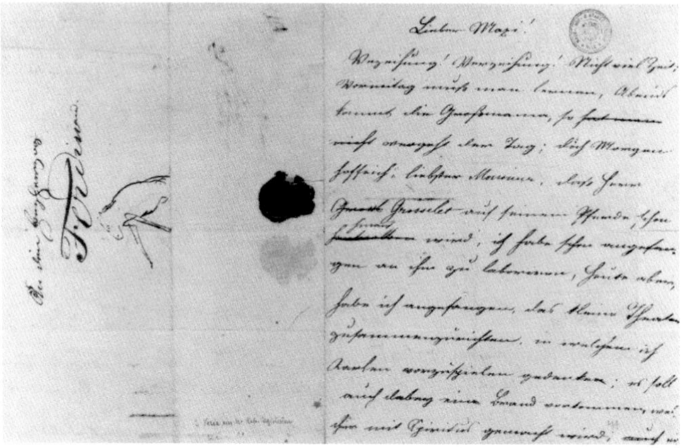

A letter from Archduke Franz to his brother Max (transcribed above).

A letter from Archduke
Franz to his brother Max.

His brother obviously
being ill, Franz uses this
letter to cheer him up by
relating a story read to
him by his tutor Carl
Count Morzin.
The story tells of a girl
travelling through the
jungle who is attacked
by monkeys and dragged
up a tree, being fed with
coconuts before finally
being released three
hours later. Franz
embellished the letter
with caricatures of
the Count and of his
Czech language teacher
Johann Wittek.

Below and top of opposite page:
Drawings from the sketch books of the thirteen-year old Archduke, 1845/46.

Although Franz was brought up to be a dutiful heir to the throne,
the drawings he made at this time offer us a rarely seen side of the fifteen-year
old Archduke. He used these pages to capture everyday situations,
as well as recording sporting and artistic impressions from the
journeys he made through Italy, Istria and Dalmatia in 1845 and 1846.
This creative and humorous work displays no evidence
of his alleged lack of imagination and pedantry.

THE YOUNG ARCHDUKE

In 1842, the twelve year old's timetable was extended to fifty hours. As well as German, French, Hungarian, Czech and Latin, he learned history, geography, law, political science, physics, chemistry, mathematics and, above all, religion. This was supplemented by dancing, riding and military drill. His view of the world was thus formed in clerical and military terms, values which were later to mark the whole of his. In the evenings, in addition to the theatre performances already mentioned, there were children's balls to prepare the Archduke for the social dance floor. As always, Franz tried to fulfil the expectations made of him and carried out his duty reliably. A fact which was little regarded at court showed, however, the weight of the pressure Franz must have felt. He complained of stomach aches over an extended period of time and was sick every day before beginning his strictly

Franz in a red uniform tunic and holding a flag.
Reproduction of a painting by Franz von Amerling, 1838.

This representation clearly demonstrates the ambitions
harboured by the energetic Archduchess Sophie to establish her
son on the Imperial throne after it became clear that Emperor
Ferdinand would not produce any heirs. She made clever use of
picture propaganda to launch her children, particularly her
eldest son, as popular public figures. This picture features an
extremely serious depiction of Franz Joseph wearing a bayonet
strap and with the unfurled flag of the Austrian Monarchy
leaning against his shoulder, intended as an indication
of the difficult task which would await him. His knapsack,
cartridge bag and helmet, symbols of the army, have been
laid aside.

Page 25 below:
Archduke Franz being
taught in the presence
of his mother, Cardinal
Rauscher, Count
Heinrich Bombelles
and Baron Gorizutti.
Lithograph by Franz
Leypold after Ferdinand
Laufberger, around 1840.

organised day. At the same time, the Archduke, although he was
sporty and brave, had to overcome his fear of large horses. His riding
master, already fearing that Franz Joseph would never learn to ride,
had not reckoned with the strong will of his pupil. Franz forced
himself to confront his fear, and the enormous strength of will and
toughness he showed finally enabled him to develop into a safe and
elegant horseman. This unbendable will, the severity he imposed
upon himself and fulfilment of duty as an overriding principle were
attributes which were to remain with him for the rest of his life.

On his thirteenth birthday, he was appointed Colonel of the
Regiment of Dragoons, and one year later he received the Golden
Fleece, the highest decoration awarded by the Austrian Royal
House.

SUCCESSION TO THE THRONE

The past years had seen an ever-greater involvement in politics on
the part of Sophie, and, in the light of the impending crisis in
the domestic political situation, she began to become openly politically active. The court fled Vienna as a result of the revolution of the
Austrian middle classes of 1848, going first to Innsbruck, before
travelling on to Olmütz, where work went on feverishly to find a
solution. Nothing could be expected of Emperor Ferdinand, and
Franz Joseph's father, Franz Karl, was also not the sort of personality
to which the necessary intelligence, energy and presence could be

God bless you, remain virtuous, God will protect you, it is right that it has come to pass! Emperor Ferdinand gives his blessing to his successor Franz Joseph in the Archiepiscopal Palace on 2 December 1848.

attributed. Thus, greatly to Sophie's satisfaction, there was increasing talk of the young Franz as successor. She had achieved her aim; her son was to be Emperor. Firstly, however, there were consultations and discussions on what name the new Emperor should take. Sophie was anxious that Franz should call himself Franz II in memory of Emperor Franz I, whom she had much admired and esteemed. The politicians, however, were resolutely opposed to this idea. One of their aims was to use the young Kaiser to signalise a new era, and, in this respect, Franz II was too directly reminiscent of the very recent past. For this reason, the double name of Franz Joseph was settled upon, »Joseph« being consciously intended to evoke memories of the great reforming Emperor Joseph II, the idea being that Franz Joseph should also represent tradition and progress in equal measure.

Sophie's hopes were fulfilled on 2 December 1848, when Emperor Ferdinand finally abdicated, Franz Karl gave up his right to the throne and Franz Joseph became Emperor of Austria at the age of eighteen. Franz Joseph had been prepared for his duty since childhood and, despite succeeding to the throne unexpectedly early, showed great restraint and confidence, although deeply moved by the occasion. Sophie described the scene in her diary as follows: *Around 8 o' clock, the family gathered in front of the Emperor in the hall, … we sat in a semi-circle, I was moved to tears by the Emperor's reading some words renouncing his right to the throne, as were Elisa-*

Emperor Franz Joseph I. Artaria, 1848.

beth and in particular Maxi, Charles and Joseph, who had known nothing about it. Schwarzenberg read out all the documents relating to this act, the two Emperors signed them. Franzi asked for the blessing of the Emperor, who embraced him, as did the Empress, the latter particularly tenderly. Our dear child knelt before Franz Karl and me and asked for our blessing. He threw himself upon my heart and embraced me for a considerable. It was so moving …

The task facing him, however, was by no means easy. From his earliest childhood, it had been drummed into Franz Joseph that he was to maintain tradition. He was not expected to display vision or summon up the necessary strength of will or courage to pursue an independent course of action, develop new thoughts or instigate change.

Franz Joseph I.
Constitutioneller Kaiser von Oesterreich etc.
seit 2 December 1848.

EMPEROR & HUSBAND

Above:
The young Imperial
married couple. Colour
lithograph by Eduard
Kaiser, 1856.

Opposite page:
Emperor Franz Joseph.
Painting by Anton
Einsle, 1848.

THE YOUNG EMPEROR
WITH BLOOD ON HIS HANDS

After the suppression of the revolution of the Austrian middle classes, Franz Joseph's succession to the throne represented a victory on the part of the forces of monarchism and conservatism and the beginning of a neo-absolutist, reactionary political policy. Only Hungary refused to recognise the new King, declaring a republic, and assistance from Russian Czarist troops was required to quash the rebellion. Surrounded by reactionary advisors, Franz Joseph committed a whole series of serious political mistakes within the first few months of his reign. The execution of the Hungarian rebels, primarily members of that country's nobility, made him many enemies in particular. In a letter to his ally the Russian Tsar, who had earnestly urged him to exercise mercy in the interests of lasting peace, Franz Joseph replied that he would have been happy to let mercy prevail as far as his own personal feelings were concerned, but that the holy duty imposed upon him to ensure the welfare of the state constrained him to adopt an extremely strict course. Franz Joseph was a man who had been taught to heed his advisors, and he acceded to the will of his military and politicians by condemning the ringleaders of the Hungarian uprising to death. The main focus of the Austrian military, especially as far as General Haynau was concerned, was to exercise revenge and divert attention from their own failings, the Russian troops having been responsible for putting down the Austrian rebellion rather than any action on their own part. As those to be executed were, in the strictest sense of the term, prisoners of war, putting them to death represented a blatant breach of the rules of war applying at the time. This was further exacerbated by the fact that nine of the generals were hanged, considered to be a particularly shameful death. The Austrian government under Prime Minister Schwarzenberg, however, sought justification in the fact that these soldiers were deserters and guilty of high treason. As if all this were not enough, the Hungarian Prime Minister Ludwig Count Batthyány was also executed. Batthyány was one of the leading Hun-

Emperor Franz Joseph.
Painting, around 1850.

garian aristocrats and had become leader of the cabinet in 1848, undertaking repeated endeavours to achieve a peaceful solution. At the outbreak of fighting, he had withdrawn to his estate. Defamatory statements to the effect that he was partly to blame for the hostilities then induced him actually to take part in the fighting against the Imperial troops. He was arrested in January 1849 and court-martialled. Although there was no evidence that he had committed high treason, he was sentenced to death by hanging. To escape this disgrace, he attempted to take his own life by slitting his throat with a dagger smuggled into prison by his mother. He was, however, discovered in time and received medical treatment before being shot the next day. The reaction across Europe was one of horror, and there was talk of judicial murder. Franz Joseph, having blindly followed his advisors, had committed one of his most serious errors. He was everywhere dubbed the young Emperor with blood on his hands, but there was no let up from his advisors. Haynau had a total of 114 death sentences carried out, and 1765 people were sentenced to long prison sentences in dungeons. His men scoured the country punishing even the most minor of misdemeanours with the severest of measures and bringing about a regime of terror. Meanwhile, the necessity for such a course of action was constantly being drummed into the Emperor. Both the Tsar and the Imperial Governor Archduke Johann appealed to him to win over the Hungarians by exercising leniency and understanding and urged him to build his foundation of power on peace and goodwill rather than on the scaffold and the gallows. All this fell on deaf ears. It is probable that Sophie's influence had a major impact on the inflexible attitude displayed by the young Emperor at this time. Her horrified reaction to his nearly being beaten to death by brewery workers in London as a result of the atrocities he had committed in Hungary demonstrate that she was clearly on Haynau's side:

In June 1852, Franz Joseph undertook a journey through Hungary, accompanied by his adjutant Hugo Freiherr von Weckbecker, who was very close to the Hapsburgs and simply addressed as Weckbecker by the Emperor. Franz Joseph was obviously an enthusiastic and courageous swimmer, Weckbecker noting in his diary: *Part of the journey from Pest-Ofen to Bazias took place by steamship (3). Because of the hot weather, the ships made a stop every afternoon at 2 o'clock for a swim in the Danube. Since His Majesty always dived in head first from the wheel house, I asked to be allowed to go first to try the depth of the water.*

The barbarity to which General Haynau was subjected in ... London are causing a general outrage and are a source of great sadness to me!

Haynau's methods did, however, ultimately become untenable, and he made the fatal error of undermining Franz Joseph's authority by refusing to obey the Emperor's order to hand over to him all those who had been pardoned. Haynau was required to submit his resignation, which eased the situation somewhat. It was, however, to be many years before any reconciliation with Hungary was possible.

ASSASSINATION ATTEMPT ON THE EMPEROR

Assassination attempt on Emperor Franz Joseph by the journeyman tailor János Libényi. Lithograph by Albrecht, after 1851.

In Austria too, there was dissatisfaction. Franz Joseph returned to absolutism, even abrogating in 1851 the constitution he himself had enacted in 1849. The Parliament in Kremsier was dissolved and leading democrats arrested. All of this served to make Franz Joseph

extremely unpopular. The negative mood culminated in an assassination attempt made on him a short time later. Whilst the Emperor was taking a walk along the Kärntner Bastei in Vienna, the Hungarian journeyman tailor János Libényi lunged at him, although he only succeeded in inflicting a superficial knife wound to the back of the head. Sophie was particularly upset and now set about taking on a more active role in her son's life. The assassination attempt brought about an initial turning point to the level of affection in which the Emperor was held. Sophie exploited the prevailing mood and put her faith in positive »headlines«. Franz Joseph was to get married and start a family.

LOOKING FOR A WIFE

Franz Joseph was not without pre-marital experience. His first love affair had been with Elisabeth Countess Ugarte, with whom he had danced at several court balls. When one evening he even withdrew with her to a private room, the court began to gossip, and Sophie put her foot down. She summoned the married countess to her, the former subsequently leaving Vienna. Archduchess Therese, the daughter of Archduke Joseph of the Palatinate of Hungary, was a more promising prospect. The fact that the beautiful Archduchess was the sister of Archduke Stephen, who has sympathised with the Hungarians during the revolution and had even been banished from the monarchy, made her unacceptable in Sophie's eyes, however. Her wish was for a marriage with a German princess, preferably one from Prussia.

Archduke Albrecht's ball: female attendees are presented to Franz Joseph. Xylograph, 1852.

In 1852, Franz Joseph travelled to Berlin and promptly fell in love with Princess Anna, the niece of King Friedrich Wilhelm IV of Prussia, who was married to a sister of Sophie's. Anna, however, was already engaged to a German Prince and Prussia rejected the approach. Sophie was so convinced of the benefits of this alliance with the house of Hohenzollern that she fought for the marriage to take place, even overlooking the fact that Anna was a Protestant. But the Hohenzollerns were not interested in an alliance with the Habsburgs. Prince William even passed the following comment on the refusal: *We Prussians congratulate ourselves that Austria has demonstrated its subjugation in our capital city without our having to cede an inch of political ground.* The extent to which this decision was influenced by Prince Bismarck's anti-Habsburg attitude is unclear. The end result was that Franz Joseph returned to Vienna without a bride.

Sophie, however, refused to give up. There were, after all, other German Princesses amongst her nieces. Princess Sidonie of Saxony not proving to be pretty enough for Franz Joseph, in 1853 Sophie invited her sister Ludowika with her daughters Helene and Elisabeth to Ischl to take part in the celebrations to mark the Emperor's birthday. Although the Bavarian branch of the Wittelsbach dynasty was not first choice for the Emperor of Austria, it was at least German and Catholic. Sophie had her eye on the elder of the two sisters as a bride for her son, the serious-minded and well brought up Helene, known in the family as Néné. But things were not to turn out as she planned.

Elisabeth, Archduchess in Bavaria, Empress of Austria. Painting by Anton Einsle, around 1858.

Field Marshal Leutnant Hugo Freiherr von Weckbecker, Assistant Adjutant to the Emperor as Colonel-in-Chief of the Kaiserjäger Regiment. Portrait by Alfred Erggelet, 1859.

Hugo Freiherr von Weckbecker, who had accompanied the Emperor to Ischl, was assigned the task of dancing with the shy Elisabeth by Archduchess Sophie, the former requiring secure leadership on the occasion of her debut at court.

In his diary, Weckbecker described how Franz Joseph had only had eyes for the delightful princess Elisabeth during the dance, something which was obvious to all present.

After the dance, he whispered to Assistant Adjutant O'Donnel: *I believe I have just danced with our future Empress,* receiving the reply: *I am also nearly certain of that.*

ENGAGEMENT IN ISCHL

Franz Joseph fell in love with the fifteen year old Sisi as soon as he saw her. Sophie wrote of this first meeting to her sister: *He was beaming, and you know how his face beams when he is happy. The dear little thing had no idea of the deep impression she had left on Franzi.* Franz Joseph had made his choice, and, although his mother asked him not to rush into things, Franz Joseph had no wish to wait any longer than was absolutely. Sophie noted in her diary: *The Emperor rhapsodised. How sweet Sisi is. She is like a blossoming almond flower, and her face is framed by a wonderful crown of hair! What lovely eyes she has, and her lips are like strawberries!*

The official engagement took place as early as 19 August. Sisi was intimidated by the attention showered on her, whereas Franz Joseph was

»Memories of Possenhofen«: Franz Joseph, Elisabeth and Duke Max on a boat trip in Bavaria. Lithograph, 1853.

deliriously happy. Although his mother was surprised by the choice her son had made, she was accepting of the timid Sisi, not, incidentally, opposing her son's selection in any way, as has so often been reported. Quite the contrary: on the occasion of her first official appearance at the birthday ball for Franz Joseph she described Sisi as *so charming, so modest, so irreproachable, so gracious ...*, although the main source of her joy was to see her son's happiness.

During the period of engagement, Franz Joseph visited Sisi in Munich and Possenhofen as often as he could, bringing presents each time, Sisi's favourite amongst these being a parrot. In October he wrote to his mother from Munich: *... to tell you how unspeakably happy I was here and in Possenhofen, where I had all the peace and quiet I needed to enjoy my good fortune. I will never be able to thank you enough, dearest mama, for being the source of such heartfelt joy. Every day I love Sisi more and I am becoming more and more convinced that no one is better suited than she ...*

Wedding announcement of the Imperial couple.

THE YOUNG IMPERIAL COUPLE

The marriage ceremony took place on 24 April 1854, but Elisabeth's expectations of her marriage were quickly dashed. Even the first few days after the wedding itself saw the two running a veritable gauntlet. They were accorded virtually no privacy. As early as the day after the wedding, the two mothers burst in whilst the newly married couple was eating breakfast together and examined them curiously. Sophie wrote in her diary: *This was followed by the usual confidential conversation every child has with its mother*, meaning nothing less than that the two mothers subjected the couple to a detailed interrogation, uncovering the secret that there had been *no fulfilment of marital duties* during the wedding night and that, when this act finally did take place, the whole court knew about it.

Franz Joseph and Elisabeth spent their honeymoon in Laxenburg, although Franz Joseph took leave of his wife early every morning to travel to Vienna to attend to government business. He did not arrive back until late in the evening, and even then diner took place within the family circle, leaving the couple with very little time to themselves. Elisabeth was disappointed, feeling homesick and lonely. Only a few weeks after her wedding, she wrote in her diary: *Oh, if only I had never left the path that would have taken me to freedom./Oh, that I never succumb to vanity along these wide roads!*

Despite the preparation she had undergone, Elisabeth could not come to terms with her new situation in life. She felt observed and spied upon and her difficulties in adapting to the ceremonial court in Vienna met with rejection. Not being a member of a royal family, not being in possession of a fortune and not having enjoyed the education of a princess, she was made to feel that she was not a marriage match of the first order. She spoke no French, even her German conversation was inhibited, halting and self-conscious and she could not dance. Her strengths, naturalness, honesty and grace, were not in demand at the Viennese court, where protocol and ceremonial rules were the guiding principles. Although Franz Joseph loved Elisabeth more than anything in the world, he abandoned her to her fears and difficulties, placing far too many affairs into the hands of his mother, thus pushing her into a role as tutor. Since Franz Joseph was Elisabeth's only point of reference during this time, her feeling intensified that he was leaving her in the lurch. It

was many years before she was able to accept her husband's behaviour. She was also not afforded the opportunity to become his confidante, a position his mother occupied throughout her life. Elisabeth was excluded from any kind of decision making or political influence from the very start, meaning that Franz Joseph and Elisabeth also had no chance of really getting to know each other, to learn to appreciate the point of view of the other or to become intimate. Added to this was the fact that, as a young girl, Elisabeth did not possess the confidence to fight for a position outside the scope of her representative duties.

The couple's first daughter, Sophie, was born on 5 March 1855. Franz Joseph

The marriage ceremony in the church of St Augustin on the evening of 24 April 1854. Lithograph, 1854.

and his mother were present at the birth, the latter describing the event in her diary: *He kissed her unceasingly, comforted her, suffered with her and looked at me after every labour pain to see if I was content.* And when Sophie was born: *The Emperor burst into tears, he and Sisi did not stop kissing, and they embraced me with the most acute tenderness.* The Imperial couple was overjoyed, and, the very next year, on 5 July 1856, Elisabeth gave birth to a second girl, Gisela.

»The Habsburgs' youngest blossom: Archduchess Sophie«. Lithograph, 1855.

CONFLICT BETWEEN ELISABETH AND SOPHIE

During this period, there was a gradual rise in the level of conflict between Elisabeth and Sophie. Sophie was used to having her way at court, including over the Emperor, and Elisabeth still had too much respect for her powerful mother-in-law who, until her marriage, had been the »first lady« at the Viennese court. Slowly, however, she began to become aware of her position. *She* was the Empress and first lady of the empire. Elisabeth's growing popularity undoubtedly played a part in this process, providing her with a greater level of self-confidence. Elisabeth began to rebel against her mother-in-law, the two women's differing views on the children's education giving rise to this. Sophie had had the nursery set up next to her apartment, but Elisabeth wished to have her children around her and now fought against having to visit her children in her mother-in-law's apartment, in a nursery which was also under her mother-in-law's control. Archduchess Sophie, however, was not motivated by hard heartedness or malice in wishing to »take away« Elisabeth's children, her primary interest always being the welfare of the Habsburg dynasty. Her view was that the place of an Empress was at the side of her husband, the consequence of this being, however, that she did not have the time to take care of her children. Franz Joseph attempted to mediate, whereupon Sophie finally gave way and the children were moved. The great shock arrived in 1857. Elisabeth now wished her children to accompany her when she travelled, and this led to a clear expression of opposition on Sophie's part, who felt that such journeys were too exhausting and dangerous for the children. This represented a further conflict between generations and a situation where two worlds collided. Sophie expected a

professional approach from an Empress. Her opinion was that
Elisabeth was no longer part of the »bourgeoisie«, that her primary
focus should be on her duty as the Empress of Austria and that this
should take precedence over her children. Elisabeth, on the other
hand, viewed herself as more of a mother than an Empress. She
wished to have her children with her and put her own personal
interests to the fore. Franz Joseph tried not to become involved in
the dispute. His loyalties were torn, a conflict which he did not wish
to resolve even if he had been in a position to do so. Although Sisi
expected unconditional support from him, she had underestimated
the power her mother-in-law wielded over her husband and had
asked too much of Franz Joseph. The Emperor remained loyal to his
mother at al times and would never have been able to defy her. His
attempt to maintain a neutral position drove a wedge between him
and Elisabeth, the latter once again succeeding in getting the better
of her mother-in-law by taking her daughters on a journey to
Hungary. Both daughters fell ill with diarrhoea and succumbed to
a high fever, resulting in the death of Sophie at the age of two,

Portrait of Franz Joseph
and Empress Elisabeth.
Miniature on porcelain,
around 1855.

The Imperial family on the terrace of Schönbrunn Palace – the only photograph of the whole family (sitting: Elisabeth with Rudolf on her lap, Gisela, Archduchess Sophie and her husband Franz Karl; standing from left to right: Franz Joseph, Ferdinand Max and his wife Charlotte, Franz Joseph's younger brothers Ludwig Viktor and Carl Ludwig, Photograph by Ludwig Angerer, 1859.

although little Gisela recovered. Franz Joseph and Elisabeth were in despair. Elisabeth blamed herself, gave up the battle with Sophie over the upbringing of the children and placed Gisela entirely in her care.

On 21 August 1858, the long wished for Crown Prince was born, he too being put under the supervision of his grandmother in the care of the Ajas, the governesses of the children's nursery.

TIME OF CRISIS

In 1858, the death of the loyal Commander-in-Chief in Italy, Field Marshal Radetzky, spelled the end of an era. In 1859, war broke out between Austria and Sardinia-Piemont, France entering hostilities on the side of the latter. After defeat at the Battle of Magenta, Franz Joseph rushed to the front to take over supreme command himself. This was to prove to be a tragic error. The decisive battle at Solferino turned into one of the bloodiest defeats ever suffered by the Habsburg army with one of the greatest losses of life. Franz Joseph had failed as a commander in the field. Criticism of the Empress also began slowly to mount. Elisabeth missed her husband, suffered from loneliness and now withdrew completely, refusing to

show herself in public. The fact that she now either shut herself in her apartment or went out riding for hours on end was taken as a sign of a lack of interest in the political and social situation confronting the monarchy, and she was now openly accused of both neglecting her duties as Empress and of failing to take care of her children. From the front line, a despairing Franz Joseph begged her to show herself in public and provide him with the support he needed: *For the sake of the love you have sworn to me, I beg you to pull yourself together and to make public appearances in the city or official visits to institutions. You have no idea how that could help me. It will act as a tonic to the people of Vienna and maintain the positive spirit I need so much.*

Although Elisabeth organised a hospital for the wounded in Laxenburg, she was seldom seen there. Despite her lack of interest in politics, she began to provide herself with information, imparting her views to Franz Joseph and attempting to offer him advice. He, however, paid little heed, and Sophie attempted to nip this intervention into her sphere of influence in the bud.

MARRIED LIFE

As Elisabeth became older and grew in confidence, the contrasting nature of the couple's personalities inevitably led to a widening of the gulf between them. Franz Joseph saw himself first and foremost as Emperor, his role as a husband being of secondary importance to him.

Meeting between Emperor Franz Josef I and Emperor Napoleon III in Villafranca, to sign an armistice and end the Italian campaign on 12 July 1859.

Emperor Franz Joseph in gala uniform. Painting by Franz Xaver Winterhalter, 1865.

Empress Elisabeth in ball gown. Painting by Franz Xaver Winterhalter, 1865.

The Imperial couple out riding. Photo montage by Emil Hartitzsch after photographs by Emil Rabending and Ludwig Angerer, 1865/66.

His overriding priority was the fulfilment of his duty, and this took precedence over any personal interests. Elisabeth took precisely the opposite view. Her reaction was to flee, taking refuge in the cult of beauty, sporting ambition, lyrical poetry and above all in intensive travel. Franz Joseph let Elisabeth go, sensing she was not happy at his side since she did not feel she was able to support him. Because he really did love her above all else, he made it possible for her to establish a self-contained and independent life for herself, although this meant that he had to live without her. Once Elisabeth had relinquished any hopes of a fulfilling marriage, and had ultimately been freed from her duties as Empress, a marriage based on friendship began to develop, probably due in no small part to the distance between the two.

SOPHIE, THE SECRET EMPRESS

When Sophie arrived in Vienna at the age of nineteen, the first thing that Emperor Franz said to her was that she needed to take control of everything her husband did. This is exactly the course of action she ultimately pursued and, since the revolution of 1848, had become known as »the only man at court«. She had succeeded in making her son Emperor and steered and guided him as long as she lived. Despite her frequent assertions that she had vowed not to become involved in affairs of state once her son had succeeded to the throne, this was not a resolution that she was to keep for long. Although the marriage of her son meant the theoretical loss of her status as the first lady at court, the reality was that nothing had changed. The young Empress had a much lesser say in what went on at court than the archduchess, the latter issuing the instructions, making the decisions and remaining convinced that it was her duty to mould Elisabeth into an Empress according to her own perceptions in the same way as she had once done with her son. Sophie's guiding principle was that the Imperial couple, and the Emperor in particular in order to emphasise the fact that he was ruler by God's grace, needed to live their lives at a distance from »normal mortals«. In her view, the main element required to maintain this mystique was meticulous compliance with court protocol. Her son knew nothing else and submitted without resistance. Sophie had not, however, reckoned with the contradictoriness of her niece. Over the course of several years, a power struggle between the two women developed, the long term result of which was that Elisabeth, although she enjoyed some victories along the way, increasingly withdrew from the Viennese court and ceded the position and influence accorded to the first lady at court to her mother-in-law. In contrast to Sophie, Sisi was not actively interested in politics and was happy to relinquish this field to her. Once the Empress had established her independence and liberated herself from her obligations, relations between the two women also improved. It took many years for Elisabeth to develop a better understanding of her mother-in-law and to recognise that she had always acted in the interests of her son and of the House of Austria in particular.

Archduchess Sophie.
Photograph by
Ludwig Angerer, 1868.

Sophie had extended her position at court rather than simply maintaining it. It was true that Franz Joseph was the Emperor, but the fact that he had been broken of the habit of independence of thought or action since his earliest childhood tended to render him the mere executor of his mother's political will. This applied across all areas of political importance, including Austria's alliance policy, its inflexible attitude towards Hungary and extending to include the reactionary policy adopted towards the church. In 1855, for example, Franz Joseph signed the Concordat which celebrated Pope

Pius IX as *the constitutional apogee of the movement for Catholic restoration against the absolutist state and liberal tendencies.* This enabled the Catholic Church to secure the unlimited influence it exerted on the whole of the educational system, Catholic marriage law and church jurisdiction of marriage being introduced. Although this medieval Concordat attracted criticism for Franz Joseph from right across Europe, Sophie was content. She was equally convinced of the need for military intervention in Italy, being the one responsible for drumming up support in Vienna for her son and emphasising the absolute necessity for the war when Franz Joseph found himself under intense political pressure in the wake of the bloody defeats at Magenta and Solferino. Sisi, on the other hand, was merely inconsolable at the separation from her husband, weeping over the tragedy of her fate and feeling herself to be unable to appear in public and

Emperor Franz Joseph takes an oath at his coronation as king of Hungary in Pest. Coloured lithography by Vinzenz Katzler, 1867.

foster support for the Emperor. Sophie resented her greatly for this. She despised people who let themselves go, expecting Elisabeth to fulfil her duties as Empress in a professional manner and to follow her own example as someone who had always predominantly been in the service of the state by subjugating her own personal interests. In effect, Sophie had achieved her aim. Although she had not become Empress of Austria officially, she had held the position in all but name since her son had succeeded to the throne. She remained Franz Joseph's most important advisor and guide, he, in turn, retaining his loyalty to her for the rest of her life.

FROM KÖNIGGRÄTZ TO THE DOUBLE MONARCHY

Franz Joseph and Elisabeth as King and Queen of Hungary. Photo montage after Emil Rabending, 1867.

Franz Joseph's popularity was far from being based on political success. Rather than becoming larger and more powerful during his reign, Austria consistently lost territory, power and influence, the annexation of Bosnia-Herzegovina in 1908 providing the only exception to this trend. After the loss of Lombardy and, ultimately, Venice, the third great setback was to occur in 1866. Franz Joseph's attempt to pursue a »Pan German« policy under Habsburg leadership was increasingly floundering due to Bismarck and Prussia's own claim to be the dominant power. The war with Prussia which resulted from this ended with a crushing defeat for Austria at Königgrätz and spelled the end of Austria's primacy within the German Confederation. Austria was weakened, and this enabled liberal forces to make a breakthrough. In March 1867, Hungarian representatives succeeded in negotiating the Compromise, which assured the Magyars a considerable degree of independence. On 8 June, Franz Joseph swore an oath on the Hungarian constitution and was, together with his wife, who had fought vehemently for Hungarian interests, officially crowned King of Hungary in the Matthias Church in Budapest. Represented by the person of the Emperor and King respectively, the two countries were now linked by a common foreign, financial, military and war policy, the Hungarian Parliament enjoying autonomy in terms of policy relating to administration, justice, culture and education. The Compromise transformed the Habsburg Empire into a double monarchy, which was accorded the name »Austro-Hungarian Monarchy« in a handwritten document by Franz Joseph.

OH IF ONLY I COULD TELL HIM EVERYTHING!«
THE EMPEROR AS A FATHER

Above:
Archduchess Marie
Valerie, the youngest of
the children of Emperor
Franz Joseph and Empress
Elisabeth. Photograph by
Emil Rabending, 1872.

Opposite page:
Emperor Franz Joseph
with Gisela and Rudolf.
Photograph by Ludwig
Angerer, around 1860.

THE DAUGHTERS GISELA AND MARIE VALERIE

The birth of Archduchess Gisela in 1856 was a time of political pressure for Franz Joseph, meaning he spent little time with his daughter. Although he endeavoured to be a good father, affairs of state always took precedence. Gisela was a straightforward and happy child, if not pretty. She had a close relationship with her brother Rudolf, with whom she grew up, as well as with her grandmother Sophie, who took on the mother role, Elisabeth mostly being away on her travels. Influenced by her grandmother, she had the utmost respect for her father, but saw him as more of an Emperor than a father. Marie Valerie, who unlike her brothers and sisters was allowed to spend most of her time with her mother and for whom thus the small amount of time in the company of her father was all the more exciting, experienced very similar sentiments. The children had learned to conceal their feelings from their father, a particular cause of suffering to the quixotic Marie Valerie, who was never able really to show her father how much she loved and admired him: *Oh, if only I could tell him everything I feel for him! If only he could sense it!* Especially Valerie, finding herself showered with the mother love Elisabeth had latterly discovered, felt drawn towards her father and thought that she had much in common with him, although the distance between them meant she never summoned up the courage to speak to him freely and openly. When she was sixteen, she euphorically recorded in her diary that she had taken breakfast with her father in his study for the first time, even being allowed to observe him at work on the following day. Franz Joseph expressed the view that it must be boring to watch him working, but for Valerie, being permitted to sit as quiet as a mouse next to her revered father for over an hour represented the apex of happiness. Franz Joseph had no idea of the great joy he was bringing to his daughter by this action. Marie Valerie was

Archduchess Gisela, the eldest daughter of Emperor Franz Joseph and Empress Elisabeth. Photograph by Ed. Ellinger, 1872.

also always afraid that her mother could be jealous and therefore only sought contact with her father when Elisabeth was away on her travels. If she was together with both her parents, she never dared to show her affection for Franz Joseph for fear of her mother's jealousy. As a grown up, Marie Valerie blamed her grandmother Sophie for her father's aloofness: ... *it was my grandmama's system to isolate Papa and his brothers and keep them away from any intimacy with the rest of the family as if they lived on an island, believing that in this way she was imbuing them with more authority over the others and protecting them from harmful influence. I now understand the reason why Papa is always so alone and takes no joy in consorting with his relatives, making him dependent on the advice of people who are often unreliable.*

The Imperial family. Photo montage, around 1870.

CROWN PRINCE RUDOLF

Franz Joseph's relationship with his only son Crown Prince Rudolf, born in 1858, was beset with difficulties from the very start. He took the clear view that his son and heir should uphold the family's military tradition, appointing Rudolf owner of the 19th Infantry Division on the day after he was born, meaning that

Right:
Crown Prince Rudolf.
Photograph, 1865.

Below:
Crown Prince Rudolf.
Photograph, 1863.

Rudolf's path in life was pre-determined from birth by his father. Like his father before him, he wore his first uniform at the age of two and, when three and a half, accompanied Franz Joseph at military parades which went on for hours. But Rudolf was not like his father. Soldiers and military ceremony tended to frighten him rather than holding any fascination. In letters to his four-year old son, Franz Joseph reminded him time and time again to display more courage and be more of a man: … *You saw the soldiers of your regiment dancing; that must have been a pretty sight to behold, yet I hear you were afraid, and that is a disgrace …* and, on his eighth birthday, Franz Joseph sent the following greeting to his son: … *I hope you will always be a source of joy to your dear mother and myself and will show a good deal of courage, manliness and industry.* To toughen up the *weakling*, as Franz Joseph called his sensitive son and prepare him for a soldier's way of life, a strict military upbringing was imposed. This, however, only made the situation even worse, turning Rudolf into a scared, nervous and sickly child and exerting a decisive influence on him in later life. His tutor Count Gondrecourt, who lacked any kind of educational intuition, decreed draconian measures such as cold water cures and military drill lasting for hours (for a seven-year old!) regardless of whether it was cold or raining and deployed such methods as having him woken at night by pistol shots. Although Franz Joseph loved his son, he found him to be too much of a namby-pamby and was firmly of the conviction that the military drill would do Rudolf good. Elisabeth, who was mostly away on her travels during Rudolf's early years and was thus only able to maintain contact with her children by letter during this time, had no idea what was going on. When, however, she returned from an extended period of absence in 1865 and saw her son again, she found Rudolf to be so scared and nervous that she described the situation as »life threatening« and expressed the view that Gondrecourt's educational methods were *virtually making an idiot* of Rudolf. She gave Franz Joseph an ultimatum: *My wish is that I receive full and unrestricted authority in all matters relating to the children, whether this be the choice of their surroundings, where they spend their time, complete control of their upbringing, in a word the final decision is to be mine alone until the moment their reach their maturity. Elisabeth. Ischl, 24 August 1865.*

Franz Joseph gave way, and Elisabeth appointed Count Latour to take over as Rudolf's tutor. He displayed a great deal of sensitivity in mentoring the Crown Prince until the conclusion of his studies in 1877, becoming a kind of »surrogate father« and remaining a friend for the rest of Rudolf's life. Latour enabled Rudolf to receive a bourgeois and liberal upbringing, turning him into an open-minded man of many interests who despised the aristocratic lifestyle. His personal circle mostly consisted of liberal minded intellectuals and academics, which meant he came under severe fire from the conservative and clerically dominated Viennese court and made many an enemy amongst politically influential circles. Rudolf complained of the isolated position of the Emperor, who relied solely on the reports of his advisors, even the newspaper articles he received to read being sub-

Franz Joseph with Crown Prince Rudolf and the male members of the House of Hapsburg in the Small Gallery at Schönbrunn Palace. Lithograph by Vinzenz Katzler, 1863.

ject to selection. This was, in effect, a two-way process of censorship, both the people and the Emperor only being permitted to read material which had been authorised by the court. *Our Emperor does not have any friends, his character and his whole being do not permit this. He stands alone in his exalted position, speaking with his servants on business affairs yet anxiously avoiding any conversation, meaning he knows very little of the way people think and feel and of the views and opinions held by the people … He believes we are currently experiencing one of the happiest periods in Austrian history, this is the official information he receives, in the newspapers he reads only the passages which have been marked in red, and is thus cut off from any form of normal human communication and from any kind of impartial advice worthy of consideration,* wrote the Crown Prince in 1881. Rudolf's political views became ever more diametrically opposed to the official policy pursued at court and forced him to live a life full of secrets. He used a cipher system to encode his political correspondence and published his political articles anonymously. Rudolf fought for many years to obtain a function befitting his capabilities, but was ignored by his father throughout his lifetime. Franz Joseph had no confidence in his son and did not hesitate in making this painfully clear to him.

Above:
Crown Prince Rudolf.
Photograph, around 1872.

Below:
Crown Prince Rudolf with his wife Stephanie of Belgium. Photograph by C. Pietzner, around 1882.

The course of his private life was just as unsatisfactory as that of his official career. In 1881, he married Stephanie of Belgium, their daughter Elisabeth, »Erzsi«, being born two years later. The initial efforts to conduct a harmonious marriage, however, were undermined over the course of the years by the contrasting personal development of the couple and by an increasing amount of debauchery on the part of the Crown Prince, the fact that Rudolf infected his wife with a sexual disease he had contracted being not the least of the reasons for its ultimate failure. Stephanie came from a staunchly Catholic dynasty and loved representation and the ceremonial life at court. Rudolf, on the other hand, took after his mother in rejecting any form of class conceit and felt most at his ease in more relaxing surroundings, such as he found in the inns of the locality.

From 1888/89 onwards, there was a dramatic deterioration in both Rudolf's state of mind and health. His failure to win the recognition of his father, his failed marriage, his incurable disease, numerous amorous adventures, alcohol and drugs all conspired to turn the thirty-year old Rudolf into a broken-hearted wreck of a man resigned to his fate. He wrote to his confidant Count Latour: *I see the slippery slope we are on and am close to the centre of action, yet can do nothing of any kind, cannot even speak up and say what I feel and think.*

On 30 January 1889, Rudolf shot himself at the hunting lodge in Mayerling, together with his final mistress, the seventeen year-old Baroness Mary Vetsera, who was prepared to die with him. Elisabeth, who was the first at court to be informed of what had happened by Joseph Count Hojos, took on the duty of conveying the news to the Emperor. Franz Joseph was deeply affected. He had been so estranged from his son that he had not recognised his despair. As always, he displayed virtually no reaction to the outside world. He had never learned to show his feelings. Marie Valerie noted in her diary: … *Our Papa was quiet, devotional, heroic and saintly. I could not look at him without crying.* And later: *Papa's almost other-worldly, pious, uncomplaining acceptance, Mama's numb pain and her belief in pre-destiny … the sight of all this is unspeakably bitter.* During the following days, Franz Joseph showed extraordinary self-control, spending the time making visits of condolence and taking part in the

Crown Prince Rudolf on his deathbed. Photograph by A. Wimmer, 1889.

whole of the ceremonies surrounding the funeral. It was not until many weeks later that he confessed to his daughter Marie Valerie *I am becoming sadder with every passing day,* something which came as a universal surprise in light of the fact that he had always been viewed as being as solid as a rock. Valerie wrote: … *But he exercised such self-control as I never would have believed.*

IMPERIAL EVERY-DAY LIFE

Above:
Emperor Franz Joseph
on his desk.
Photograph, 1909.

Opposite page:
Study room of Emperor
Franz Josef at the
Hofburg with
a painting of Empress
Elisabeth by Franz Xaver
Winterhalter (1864).
Photograph by Raimund
Stillfried von Rathenitz,
around 1900.

THE EMPEROR'S DAILY ROUTINE

The Emperor's day began without exception at 4 o' clock in the morning when his personal body servant, whose room was directly next to the Emperor's bedroom, entered and greeted him with the words *I prostrate myself at Your feet, Your Majesty, good morning.* Franz Joseph rose immediately, enquired as to the weather and commenced his morning toilet. He then dressed, normally in the simple uniform of an infantry lieutenant, and knelt on the prie-dieu next to his bed for a short morning prayer. He then proceeded directly to his desk and began to work on the neatly ordered files. During this time, his personal physician Court Counsellor Kerzl would arrive for his morning visit and enquire as to the Emperor's health. At five o' clock, his valet finally brought his breakfast tray, containing coffee, butter, pastries and, apart from on fasting days, ham. His daily work then began.

At nine o' clock, his General Adjutant would arrive for an audience, followed by the Head of the Military Chancellery and the

Franz Joseph attached no importance to splendid furnishings – quite the contrary. His modest lifestyle was also reflected in the design of his living quarters at the Hofburg Palace, which were uniformly decorated in the style of the Second Rococo. Red silk damask, the so-called »court damask«, was stretched across the walls, the furniture being white-gold in reference to the era of Maria Theresia, made of palisander and walnut and also covered with red silk damask. The Bohemian lead crystal chandeliers were made by Lobmeyr, using candles until the end of the nineteenth century, the Imperial apartments finally being electrified in 1891. The rooms were practically furnished. The Emperor himself, for example, slept in a simple bed made of iron, varnished to look like walnut.

High Court Master. There were then visits from ministers, the General Ministers Council taking place twice a week in the conference room.

His personal body servant for the last twelve years, Eugen Ketterl, reported that in his later years, Franz Joseph set great store by learning the truth and appreciated honesty and frankness. He was only prone to becoming angry with his valet if he discovered that an attempt had been made to keep things secret from him or hush a matter up. He also displayed an interest in the prevailing mood of the population.

Ketterl reported that the Emperor particularly liked to learn what was going on when getting dressed in the morning. Whether this had anything to do with the accusations made by his son and Rudolf's tragic suicide we cannot be certain. Ketterl's attempts to liberate the Emperor from the forced isolation imposed on him by the court made him far from a popular figure with the court camarilla. Sophie had enforced this isolated position on her son until the very last, and resistance to the idea had never crossed Franz Joseph's mind.

It was not until late in his reign that Ketterl brought him such things as newspapers and articles otherwise strictly kept from the Emperor, conveying to him much that he would never have heard or seen in the ordinary course of events.

Luncheon was served at midday precisely. It consisted of soup, beef with vegetables, beef-steak or poultry and a glass of »Spaten« beer. Franz Joseph always ate at his desk so as to avoid wasting valuable time and enabling him

Valet Friedrich Spannbauer lays out the Emperor's luncheon. Drawing by Theo Zasche, around 1900.

Valet Rudolf Rottner in the Emperor's bedroom. Drawing by Theo Zasche, around 1900.

The Emperor's cigar case and cigar holder.

to continue work directly afterwards. Ketterl was often angered that members of the Cabinet Chancellery chose this short lunch break of all times to disturb Franz Joseph with »urgent« reports and thought up an unusual measure to enable the Emperor to enjoy a short luncheon break: without further ado, he locked the study door.

In the afternoon, the Emperor returned to his files, in-tray on the left, out-tray on the right. The only »vice« Franz Joseph persisted with was smoking. He loved »Virginians«, actually a cheap cigar which was also smoked by the cabmen in Vienna. It was not until many years later that he had to switch to lighter brands, such as Regalia Media, on the orders of his doctors.

At six o' clock, the formal family dinner took place, to which all family members who were in the Hofburg Imperial Palace or Schönbrunn Palace at the time were invited. Even dinners with close family members followed a strict protocol, very similar to that used at court banquets.

Ministers' Council in the Emperor's conference room. Drawing by Theo Zasche, around 1900.

Once Gisela and Marie Valerie were married and were no longer in the house, and especially after the death of Elisabeth, even the Emperor found the family dinners to be an unpleasant and stiff affair during which the atmosphere was generally tense. Franz Joseph did not like very many of the members of his family who lived in Vienna, and, since he perceived the behaviour of many of the Archdukes to be incorrect, he did not wish to see most of them at all, and of those he did wish to see, many were welcome only at infrequent intervals. Finally, the family dinners were cancelled altogether. In his later years, the Emperor preferred to eat

in his study in the company of Katharina Schratt. Franz Joseph had a predilection for simple dishes such as boiled beef and pancakes and did not attach any importance to exquisite haute cuisine. In summer, especially when in Ischl, he even favoured an evening meal consisting of soured milk and black bread. At nine o' clock in the evening, the Emperor usually went to bed, only staying up later for official occasions such as court balls and gala dinners.

THE FORMAL BANQUET

Anyone invited to a formal banquet received an »Invitation to the Table of His Majesty«, detailing the date and time of arrival at the Hofburg Imperial Palace, the place where invited guests were to assemble and the dress code.

When all the guests had gathered, the Emperor was informed and joined them. After brief greetings, the party went in to dinner.

The Emperor always sat in the centre of the table opposite his guest of honour, ladies and gentlemen being seated alternately. Conversation was only permitted with a guest's immediate neighbour, general conversation and speaking in a larger group only being allowed after dinner, when the gentlemen usually withdrew to the smoking salon, smoking in the presence of ladies being considered impolite. The rumour that guests got nothing to eat at court, the Emperor him-self eating so little and at such speed that the dishes were cleared away almost as soon as they were served, must be considered

Formal family dinner.
Drawing by Theo Zasche, around 1900.

Top:
Menu for a family dinner on 18 August 1909.

Laid table in the dining room at the Hofburg Palace in Vienna (below) and a dessert table at the time of Emperor Franz Joseph, Viennese porcelain flower patterned plates, Grand Vermeil cutlery and a mousseline glass service by J. & L. Lobmeyr (right).

The table was always decorated with gilded centrepieces embellished with confectionary and flowers, although the later needed to be unscented. The cutlery was placed on the right hand side and was laid out from the outside in. The table was laid for one course at a time, a separate wine being served for each course, which naturally necessitated a different glass to be provided each time. Beside the cutlery were the menu and a personal salt-cellar. The guests were served by groups of four men, each group being responsible for four guests and the Emperor being served at the same time by his huntsman or duty valet. The serving footman proffered the dishes and plates, the wine footman the drinks and the sauce man served both sauces and vegetables. The fourth footman changed the plates. The whole serving staff operated under the supervision of the Court Table Inspector, carrying out their work precisely and above all without making a sound. Although Franz Joseph himself was not a connoisseur of wine, the court cellars had a wide variety of wines in stock. Court banquets usually began with oysters, served with Chablis, followed by a soup to which beer was the accepted accompaniment, the hors d'oeuvre coming with Rhine wine, fish with Bordeaux, the steak course with champagne, roast meat with or poultry with sherry or Madeira, dessert with Hungarian Tokai or Lacrima Christi and, finally, the black coffee with a selection of liqueurs. To enable the dishes to be kept warm and served fresh at all times, they were transported from the court kitchen to the apartments where the banquet was taking place in heated thermal boxes and kept warm in neighbouring serving rooms using coal fired, and later, gas heaters. A course was considered finished as soon as the Emperor laid down his cutlery. Since the dishes were immediately cleared away at this point, Franz Joseph always took care to be a polite host by eating slowly and only putting down his cutlery when his guests had finished eating. A court banquet consisted of between nine and thirteen courses, but only lasted around fifty-five minutes.

apocryphal. The Emperor naturally paid due heed to his guests, General Mendl-Burghardt, himself several times a guest at court recalling: ... *it was often said that guests were not*

View of the great court kitchen. Photograph, around 1900.

able to eat their fill at court banquets, since one course followed another at lightning speed. I must firmly refute this allegation, however; there was sufficient time for ample enjoyment of the food which was served ...

Gala dinner in the Great Gallery at Schönbrunn Palace. Painting by Fritz l'Allemand, 1867.

AN AUDIENCE WITH HIS MAJESTY

General audiences, to which every citizen without exception had access, took place twice a week. These audiences, which were advertised in the *Wiener Zeitung*, afforded everyone the opportunity to approach the Emperor with his personal suits. An appointment had to be requested in the Cabinet Chancellery and the reason for seeking an audience with the Emperor stated. The publicist Franz Anton Rosental wrote: ... *there is no other monarch who acts as a true father of his country by permitting even the poorest of his subjects to obtain an audience with him without difficulty and the civil servants treat even the most modest of petitioners in the best way, displaying appropriate attention and condescension ...*

Those seeking an audience had to present themselves either in military, civil servant or court uniform, a black tailcoat or dark full length dress respectively, or in national costume. The vast majority of citizens from country areas in particular, who did not possess any kind of tailcoat or uniform, presented themselves in

Emperor Franz Joseph's pince-nez.

The Court Ball
in the Hofburg.
Watercolour by
Wilhelm Gause,
around 1906.

national costume. This was unusual, but Franz Joseph attached importance to being able to hear the concerns of any of his subjects and did not wish this access to be restricted by the dress code. Franz Joseph received an average of a hundred persons in a morning into the 1890's, the figure only being reduced by half when he was very elderly.

Those receiving an audience ascended the Emperor's staircase into the Audience Anteroom, where a senior court commissioner checked the names and ordered them according to rank, an assistant adjutant having the task of entertaining those waiting until they were admitted. The reasons for submitting a petition were multifarious and mostly of a purely personal nature. Petitioners came to offer thanks for honours they had received and to introduce themselves if they had

been appointed to an official position; anyone in distress could ask for financial support or for mercy for family members who had been unjustly or too harshly punished.

Contemporary accounts provide us with a vivid picture of the events and prevailing mood within this room, those about to receive an audience nervously practising over and over again the sentence they had rehearsed and wished to present to the Emperor to avoid the situation of letting their awe get the better of them to the extent of unable to utter a single word at the decisive moment. Then the great moment arrived. Most audiences only lasted a few minutes, a nod of the head from the Emperor signalling that time was up.

Eugen Ketterl in the Emperor's uniform cloakroom. Drawing by Theo Zasche, about 1900.

MEMOIRS OF HIS PERSONAL BODY SERVANT

Eugen Ketterl came to the court in 1892 at the age of thirty-five on the recommendation of Count Bellegarde, whose castle administrator he had been. For two years, he served in the banqueting chamber before being appointed the Emperor's personal body servant in 1894. His memoirs not only afford us the opportunity to obtain an intimate view of the Emperor but also shed light on a wide range of extraordinary facts relating to his everyday life. Ketterl described the Emperor as follows: *The Emperor was most gracious to us all and was possessed of an extraordinary politeness ... he never issued orders, always requesting services and proffering his thanks when the article asked for was handed to him or the successful conclusion of a* task was reported … His Majesty had an enormous amount of self-control. I never saw the Emperor moody or irascible, he was never heard to shout. As »Emperor«, he always felt inhibited and harboured the thought that to let himself go would not be in the interests of the Empire. His outward appearance was always quiet and controlled, regardless of any inner turmoil he may have been experiencing.

»THAT COSTS TOO MUCH«

The first thing that struck Ketterl was the Emperor's frugality. An initial indication of this came when the Emperor undertook a journey to Cap Martin, where he was to spend some days with Elisabeth. He refused to use the separate court train, preferring to have a salon carriage attached to the scheduled train. *That would cost too much* was his succinct comment. Upon taking up his duties, Ketterl was thoroughly staggered by the generally modest nature of the Emperor's living conditions. *Anyone who imagines that the rich and mighty Emperor of Austria must have an enormous collection of exquisitely made linen and shoes to call his own is very wide of the mark. The wardrobe of the »Count of Hohenembs«, the name used by the Emperor when he travelled incognito, was more than meagre … an exceptionally out-of-date tailcoat and an informal tailcoat which had already belonged to history there were scarcely more than two suits with jackets which were wearable … His linen was made of simple calico and was not even up to the standard of mine …*

Campaign uniform of an Austrian field marshal with Hungarian markings.

Initialled handkerchief belonging to the Emperor.

The Emperor was completely indifferent to the dictates of fashion. Although Franz Joseph attached great importance to the correctness of all the details and accessories of his enormous number of uniforms, he paid no heed to his civilian clothing, as Ketterl attested thinking nothing of wearing a blue tie with a green jacket. He went even further, even despising being fashionably dressed: *The day before yesterday at nine o' clock, I received a visit from the famous tailor Frank to review and add to my civilian wardrobe and allow me to present myself on the Riviera as a budding dandy,* he wrote to Elisabeth in 1894. One episode recorded by Ketterl in his memoirs throws a particular light on the good nature and flashes of humour Franz Joseph was sometimes capable of as well as confirming his views on fashion: *Before we even arrived, I was forced to ascertain that His Majesty was by no means as well equipped as should have been the case. As far as His Majesty's wardrobe was concerned, particularly regarding the civilian clothing, the situation was dismal. The former personal body servant Hornung, whose job it should have been to maintain the clothing, was an old man of eighty who paid no attention to anything and never did a hand's turn, the very fact that the Monarch found the services of this slow and stubborn old man acceptable being ample proof of the Emperor's modest demands. Just to give one example: I was searching through the linen box, the Emperor having requested a certain pair of uniform trousers. We abandoned all other activities, sorted through all the boxes and, as if cursed, the trousers were nowhere to be found, sweat was breaking out on my forehead and, even though I told myself I bore no responsibility for what had happened in the past, it was highly embarrassing to fail in the first duty I had been assigned. I immediately summoned assistance and finally an inventive servant believed he had found the solution, or I should say a fortuitous excuse*

Emperor Franz Joseph's personal body servant Eugen Ketterl. Photograph, around 1905.

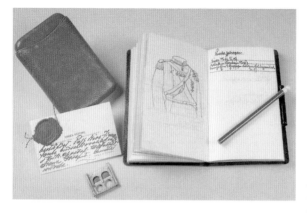

Emperor Franz Joseph's uniform book, in which Eugen Ketterl kept detailed records of when the Emperor had worn which uniforms, next to a cigar case complete with cigar cutter belonging to the Emperor.

in the idea of imparting the news that the trousers had been eaten by moths. The Emperor kept a straight face, merely shaking his head and saying thoughtfully: »*Terrible, and they didn't even leave the buttons behind!*«

Ketterl was also astonished that the Emperor of Austria should only possess one fur coat, a Russian sable which had been a gift from Tsar Alexander II, a friend of Franz Joseph's. The Tsar was naturally aware of Franz Joseph's preference for uniforms and had had a grey cover and military buttons added to the fur coat, which the Emperor wore on all in journeys year in year out. When Ketterl politely drew the Emperor's attention to the fact that this fur coat had had twenty years of use, had probably now served its purpose and that consideration should be accorded to the purchase of a new coat, Franz Joseph was horrified, saying *But that would cost too much money!* Ketterl insisted on a new fur coat, but the decision to spend 800 guilders was not an easy one for the Emperor, since he held the view that all purchases relating to his own personal use were superfluous and therefore needed to be avoided.

In contrast to this, the collection of foreign uniforms was magnificent. Since it was known that Franz Joseph always received visiting foreign princes in the uniform of their countries, it had become the custom for visitors to present the Emperor with their most magnificent national uniforms. Ketterl did not omit to mention, however, that a large number of the »diamond« medals presented to the Emperor contained in many cases false gems, although he did emphasise that the noble donors may have known nothing about this, and that their suppliers had counted on the discretion of the Emperor of Austria.

When a piece of clothing or other objects for the Emperor's private use had undergone so much wear and tear that even the thrifty Franz Joseph accepted that they needed to be rejected, the articles were not thrown away but either stamped with a letter A or marked by the valet to show they were surplus to requirements before being stored separately and sold in a grand auction at Christmas. This system applied to socks, shirts, brushes, combs, soap remnants or even the Emperor's old toothbrushes. The proceeds of the auction went to the court servants.

»... AND THE LIVER DUMPLINGS HOPPED GOOD NATUREDLY OVER THE CARPET ...«

Especially in comparison to his wife, Franz Joseph was a particularly uncomplicated, modest and unaspiring monarch. He was so accustomed to maintaining the tried and tested tradition that the idea of insisting certain things be done in accordance with his will never seems to have occurred to him, never, for example requesting a particular dish when the fancy took him. It also never entered his head to have something to eat brought to him between the fixed mealtimes if necessary, preferring to go hungry instead. He took the view that the kitchen and especially the cook were not set up to fulfil such desires and had no wish to create. If the memoirs of his faithful body servant are anything to go by, Franz Joseph did not seem to be at all as boring and pedantic as he is customarily portrayed. Quite the contrary: he communicates to us the image of a good-hearted, sympathetic and above all human Emperor. One day, for example, the already very elderly valet Hornung had an accident, Ketterl describing the incident as follows: *Old Hornung, who was terribly jealous towards me, still refused to let anyone else serve His Majesty with the*

Personal possessions of the Emperor: a house frock coat, called a »Bonjourl« (shortened form of a general's coat), a house cap, handkerchiefs, a cigar holder, spurs, a purse and visiting cards accompanied by an autograph affidavit by personal body servant Eugen Ketterl and the Emperor's personal gun loader Johann Hoschtalek.

luncheon tray. Tremulous and seething with inner anger as usual, in his overeagerness the eighty year old stumbled. The soup tureen overbalanced, causing the soup to flow onto the floor and the liver dumplings to hop good-naturedly across the carpet. Through the door, I heard the deeply shocked Hornung stammer »A thousand pardons, I prostrate myself before Your Majesty ...« – »That's the last thing we need« countered the Emperor with sympathetic anger, »I already have the liver dumplings on the floor before me as it is.«

THE »BATHWASHER«

Washstand in the Emperor's bedroom in Schönbrunn Palace.

Franz Joseph displayed a similar level of sympathy and humour in an incident which was came about on account of the astonishing fact that The Emperor did not have his own bathroom. As already mentioned, Franz Joseph strictly rejected any form of personal luxury, the fact that he even forewent the convenience of a bathroom bearing testimony to the absolute modesty of his demands and demonstratively Spartan lifestyle, although this was not something he sought to impose on anyone else in the family.

Ketterl described the Emperor's washstand, a folding wooden piece of furniture which held far too little water, as *so terribly primitive* that Franz Joseph was constantly bruising himself on the sharp corners and edges. As ever, the Emperor refused to order a new one, and Ketterl was forced to resort to a cunning ruse to get him to agree to the change. He claimed to have discovered a beautiful English washstand in a far-flung room of the Schönbrunn Palace which would be suitable in every way. Franz Joseph having agreed to the exchange, Ketterl ordered a beautiful, open washstand from Wahliß, and the Emperor of Austria finally had adequate washing facilities.

The Emperor took his daily morning bath in a bathtub made of caoutchouc. He had the assistance of his own bathroom servant, although the unusual hours of duty sometimes caused difficulties with these servants. Ketterl describes the following exquisite scene:

The bath mat had already been prepared in the bedroom the evening before, and now the tub and the »bathwasher« swung into

action. We always had a great deal of trouble with this bathroom
servant. Although he did not support the throne, this man, whom des-
tiny had appointed to the most intimate personal contact with the
Emperor of Austria, felt he was entitled to seek support himself from the
wearer of the crown. This came about in the following way. Getting up
at 3 o' clock in the morning in winter is not particularly pleasant and
not everyone's cup of tea. »If I am to be called to duty at this hour of the
night«, reasoned this bold man, »then there is only one way to overcome
the difficulties of having to get up so early, and that is not to go to bed.«
Deed followed word. Our »bathwasher« thus became a regular and
hard drinking guest in the nearby »Vierstöcklkeller«. He drank so as to
avoid falling asleep and, although the method was successful in this
respect, he began to suffer from a lack of balance both mentally and
physically. Thus it was that in this condition he also forgot the awe due
to the monarch, making several morning appearances before the
Emperor's rubber bath hardly in a fit state for an audience. The
unusual sight of this subject, who certainly was not lacking in original-
ity, going about his duties whilst requiring a considerable level of assis-
tance himself, amused the Emperor at first, and he simply com-
mented that »an eye should be kept on him for a while«,
since he probably »couldn't hold his drink«. However,
when the bathwasher's lack of stability caused him for the
third time to grip His Majesty's arms so tightly that it
seemed the small bathing facility, small as it was, was on
the point of having two occupants, this spelled the end of the man's
service. His In his benevolence, however, His Majesty did not have him
sent away, simply requesting he be allocated other duties which would
obviate the necessity of having to
keep himself awake in the »Vier-
stöckl« until three o' clock in the
morning.

A house cap and
the travelling set of
the Emperor.

The next thing Ketterl
tackled was what he perceived to
be the untenable situation of the
Emperor's lack of toilet facilities.
Whereas Empress Elisabeth had
had her own modern bathroom
since 1876 and a toilet with water
closet since at least 1885, both in
the Schönbrunn and Hofburg

Palaces the Emperor was obliged to make his way through three separate rooms to reach his chamber pot. Ketterl started by having the chamber pot placed between the double doors of the bedroom in Schönbrunn, a closet with flush being later installed in the same location, whereas in the Hofburg he even had a part of his own servant's room partitioned off to create a separate room for the Emperor's toilet.

»KETTERL, KETTERL, SOMEONE WISHES TO SPEAK TO ME, HAVE A LOOK WHO IT IS!«

We have already seen that the Emperor was no friend of technical innovation. He took the same view of the invention of the telephone, firmly refusing to tolerate any such apparatus on his desk. He did, however, finally relent to the extent of allowing a telephone to be installed in his apartment at least. The occasion was the marriage of Crown Princess Stephanie to Count Elmer Lonyay in 1900. The wedding was to take place in Miramare, and the idea was that the Emperor should convey his congratulations by telephone. Unbelievably, no more suitable location could be found than the partitioned off part of the valet's room which served as the Emperor's toilet! Ketterl reported on the subsequent »amusing« scene: *The*

The Emperor's toilet in Schönbrunn Palace.

Emperor happened to be in the partitioned off room when the telephone rang. "What will he do now?" I thought to myself as I stood outside the door. "Wait" called His Majesty. The telephone, however, continued to ring. "Wait!" thundered the Emperor, seemingly almost in the belief that the person calling at the other end of the line must hear him. But the telephone paid no heed and rang for a third time, and this time the Emperor cried out in despair: "Ketterl, Ketterl, someone wishes to speak to me, have a look who it is!

It turned out only to be the coachman who wished to enquire if the Emperor would care to drive out in an open or closed carriage, the weather being uncertain …

»Quick, he should come as he is!«

As far as dealing with his staff was concerned, Franz Joseph was generally an uncomplicated sort of person, not, for example, requiring any formalities from his personal servants as they went about their duties. When he walked through his apartment in the early morning whilst the rooms were being tidied up, the servants did not take the slightest notice of his presence, neither greeting the Emperor nor interrupting their work for even a moment.

The assertion that Franz Joseph reacted highly sensitively were anyone to appear before him not wearing a tailcoat is also not correct. This only applied to Ministers at the Ministers Council, his personal physician Court Counsellor Kerzl wore a jacket or a frock coat whilst making his morning visits, and other persons called to the Emperor's presence early in the morning knew he took the time of day into account. They even had fun complying with the order *Quick, he should come as he is!* as literally as possible. Thus it often came to pass that counsellors on duty and court secretaries from the Military and Cabinet Chancellery reported to the Emperor dressed only in their nightshirts, over which that had artistically draped a cloak, or, in the event that their morning toilet routine was more advanced, appearing before him at least with their ties hanging down backwards.

High Court Master Rudolf Prince Liechtenstein with Emperor Franz Joseph. Print from a drawing by Theo Zasche, 1897/98.

THE EMPEROR'S PRIVATE LIFE

Above:
Emperor Franz Joseph
in Lederhose and with
walking stick. Photograph
by Charles Scolik,
around 1900.

Opposite page:
Emperor Franz Joseph and
Empress Elisabeth during
a stay on Cap Martin
in Mentone.

CAREFREE DAYS ON THE CÔTE D'AZUR

Franz Joseph had very little time as a private citizen. His whole day was taken up with affairs of state and, even though he took a few days' holiday per year, he continued to work during this time too. He was so set in his ways that it seemed he was unable to imagine any other kind of daily routine. One of the very few private trips he allowed himself was a few days on the French Riviera in the company of Elisabeth during the 1890's. Franz Joseph began this »holiday« by taking a mountain of files onto the train with him, on which he proceeded to work during the journey, an accompanying adjutant returning the processed files to Vienna and collecting new ones, which provided the Emperor with at least a few days off.

Franz Joseph and Elisabeth both looked forward to this brief private holiday on the Côte d'Azur. The Empress travelled on a few days ahead to prepare everything for Franz Joseph's arrival. She sought out new routes for walks and organised excursions and cosy evenings together, the couple being afforded the rare opportunity of spending the latter quite alone. Elisabeth's companion Irma Sztáray wrote of the Empress' preparations: *When ever we saw anything lovely on our walks, the immediate reaction was: »We'll show that to the Emperor.« If we had something nice to eat: »Make a note of that, the Emperor will enjoy it.« The whole of her thoughts was devoted to him throughout these hours of joyful*

Elisabeth departing: commemorative postcard, 1898.

Als sie Abschied nahm!

Die Abreise der Kaiserin von Oesterreich.

16. IX. 1898.

expectation, everything else being of secondary importance. »*It is so rare for the Emperor to allow himself a brief holiday, let us do everything we can to make these few days as pleasant as possible for him.*« When few short days of harmony were over, each once again went their separate ways.

Even after so many years, such partings were painful for Franz Joseph. After the two met briefly in 1897, he wrote: *Édes szeretett lelkem,* (my sweet, dear soul) *After such an interminably brief time together, we return to the restrictions of written correspondence. This is sad, but unfortunately unavoidable. I am most affected by this latest parting from you …*

The Emperor's briefcase.

»MY DEAR ANGEL« – LETTERS TO EMPRESS ELISABETH

Throughout his life, Franz Joseph loved his wife above all else and fulfilled her every wish. It was only his support – including financial assistance! – that enabled her to lead her independent life and finance her costly travels and accommodation costs, al of which swallowed up enormous sums of money. Elisabeth respected Franz Joseph and held him in high esteem, after the death of Archduchess Sophie in May 1872 even becoming a confidante with whom he could also discuss politi-

Elisabeth in the early morning light. Copy by E. Riegele from the original by Franz Xaver Winterhalter, 1864.

cal matters, although this development sadly came too late. The couple saw each other more often than is generally made out. Even in the later years, when Elisabeth was often on her travels, they met regularly, spending in spring some weeks in the Hermes Villa in Vienna, mostly in the company of their daughters, the summer in Ischl, and a few days in Hungary in autumn. When Elisabeth was away, they wrote nearly every day. These are certainly not superficial letters merely to fulfil a duty, as is sometimes suggested. They provide detailed descriptions of their daily lives, incidents which occurred and of their thoughts. Elisabeth told of her travels, Franz Joseph providing news of the children, his daily business and using the letters to pour out his feelings of longing for her. Franz Joseph's letters always began with *My dearest angel Sisi, My dear angel* or *Beloved Sisi* and ended with *Your deeply loving* (or *lonely*) *little man*, this later being replaced simply by *Your little one*. In 1866, he wrote: *My dear angel! Now I am once again alone with my troubles and am longing for you. Come back soon to visit me, if your strength and health allow it that is, because even though you*

> *How happy I would be if I were able to grant your wish and enjoy all this with you in peace and quiet and be able to see you again after such a long parting; sadly I can not think of this at the moment, because, quite aside from the great difficulties of the political situation, the whole of the second half of September is already occupied with jubilee celebrations, church consecrations and visiting the exhibition ...*
>
> Franz Joseph in in his last letter to Elisabeth on 9 September 1898.

were so cross and cruel, my love for you is still endless and is such that I cannot be without you .... He found the times following the days they spent together particularly hard. In 1893, he wrote: *... I am only slowly becoming accustomed to my loneliness, and am still reliving the moments spent with you at breakfast and the evenings together and, despite the coldness of your rooms, I have already twice found myself in your rooms whilst on my way to the Bellaria and, although all the furniture is covered up, everything reminds me so painfully of you...*

THE HUNTER

The only pleasure Franz Joseph allowed himself in his capacity as a private citizen was hunting, an activity in which he really blossomed. He loved to stalk his prey, enjoy nature and find peace and quiet and a change of scene away from the monotonous everyday life at court. He was a passionate hunter of wild boar and big game, deer, chamois and wild pigs interesting him more than partridges or rabbits. Franz Joseph was, however, a real hunter rather than a trophy collector. He despised the *mass slaughter*, as he termed it, practised by his nephew and later heir Franz Ferdinand, once commenting: *Recently, Archduke Franz Ferdinand made several hundred kills in the Lainzer Park, incomprehensible, they are simply*

Emperor Franz Josef with a twelve point antler deer near Bad Ischl. Photograph, 1912.

pets, *that is absolutely not the act of a true hunter.* According to his valet Ketterl, it is not true that he had people to drive the game in front of his shotgun. Quite the contrary was the case. As an old man, he often tackled climbs of up to an hour and a half in duration to reach hunting grounds at considerable altitude, always carrying his own gun. In his early years, he used single-bore, small calibre drop barrel rifles, the so-called »Ischler Stutzen« without repeating action. In later years, he preferred a Lancaster double-barrelled rifle, sometimes using a gun with telescopic sights. Whilst hunting, Franz Joseph always wore the traditional costume of a Styrian big game hunter, consisting of a grey jacket with a stand-up collar, a sash, a green waistcoat, chamois leather trousers, grey woollen socks, a grey felt hat with chamois beard or blackcock feather and rough, cobbled shoes, the older the better. And the same applied to the »chamois«, which needed to be as old and greasy as possible. Ketterl related: *In time, the trousers became so worn, greasy and shiny that they would not have looked out of place on the next best woodcutter. But a tough struggle was always require before His Majesty would agree to the purchase of new »leathers«, and then*

Opposite page:
Emperor Franz Joseph in hunting dress. Photograph, around 1900.

Left:
Emperor Franz Joseph. Photograph, 1910.

Count Wurmbrand is holding a speech in Ischl for Emperor Franz Joseph. Photograph, around 1910.

the new pair had to be rubbed up and down the stairs and subjected to a whole range of other methods to make them artificially old and worn before he put them on, otherwise they seemed too dandified to the noble gentleman. The Emperor also never went hunting without his long hunting stick or alpenstock. The most important thing of all to Franz Joseph, as befitted a true huntsman, was that his knees were uncovered no matter what the weather, never being protected by long johns when it was cold.

Emperor Franz Joseph.
Photograph, around 1914.

Blows of fate

In the course of his long life, Franz Joseph had to bear several cruel blows of fate. The early death of his much loved first daughter Sophie, on whom he doted, was certainly a traumatic experience. When she fell ill, he remained with Elisabeth at her bedside and, after they had looked on in despair for eleven hours at the death of their child, he telegraphed to his mother from Budapest: *Our little one is an angel in heaven. After a long struggle, she finally passed away peacefully at half past nine. We are devastated.* Franz Joseph kept a small portrait of his daughter on his desk for the rest of his life, and even though he never spoke of it, he never forgot his painful loss.

Shortly before Elisabeth's death in September 1898, Marie Valerie noted in her diary: ... *Memories are re-emerging – pain long past – memories also of the baby, taken more than 40 years ago, and about which Papa now asks, wishing to preserve the memories but not see them. I think that is the first time I have heard him speak of the »baby« ...*

Emperor Max of Mexico

The next bitter blow for Franz Joseph was the execution of his younger brother Max, the most talented, imaginative and popular of all the brothers, interested in science from an early age and a lover of foreign lands and travelling. Since any kind of academic career was completely out of the question for an Archduke, he was finally trained as a rear admiral in the Austrian navy and was Governor of the Kingdom of Lombardy-Venice between 1857 and 1859. As the second born, he had no opportunity of fulfilling his ambitions within the Aus-

Archduke Ferdinand Maximilian, Emperor Franz Joseph's brother and his junior by two years. Photograph by G. Malovich, Trieste, 1864.

trian Monarchy. In 1864, with the support of the United States and not least because he was egged on by his ambitious wife Charlotte of Belgium, he accepted the offer of Napoleon III to become Emperor of Mexico.

Despite the difficult political situation and in the face of warnings from the Austrian advisors, the couple travelled to Mexico and took the crown. A short time later, both France and the USA withdrew their support, leaving Maximilian with virtually no chance of controlling the unrest within the country. He was finally

besieged in the Querétaro Fortress by rebels under the command of the Mexican lawyer of Indian descent Benito Juarez and taken prisoner. He was offered a chance to escape, but refused.

He was sentenced to death by a military court and, on 19 June 1867, as a symbol of the victory of the Mexican independence movement over the vested interests of European imperialism, he was executed by firing squad. His body was accompanied to

The execution of Emperor Maximilian of Mexico on 18 June 1867. Painting by Edouard Manet, 1867.

Trieste by his friend Admiral Tegetthoff on the »Novara«, the first ship he had commanded, and was finally interred in the Imperial crypt in Vienna. In contrast to his mother, who was never able to get over this loss, Franz Joseph, having had it drilled into him to exercise self-control and conceal his emotions, displayed little reaction. He did not show his mourning to anyone, not even to his closest intimates, which led to the absurd rumours that he was not particularly sorry about his brother's death because the latter would have posed a threat to him as a potential heir to the throne.

The last photograph of Empress Elisabeth (together with Countess Sztáray) before her death, taken on 3 September 1898 in Territet.

DEATH OF THE EMPRESS

Only nine years after the tragic suicide of his son, a further tragedy overtook Franz Joseph. In September 1898, Elisabeth had been spending some weeks in Switzerland. On 10 September, on the way from the hotel in Geneva to the quayside, she was stabbed to death with a sharpened file by the Italian anarchist Luigi Lucheni. At first, no one noticed the fatal injury, not even Elisabeth herself. Lucheni had stabbed the Empress right through the heart, and she was slowly bleeding to death internally. Elisabeth was able to go on board, but fainted after she had been on the ship for a short while. Attempts were made to revive the Empress with Eau de Cologne and a piece of sugar dipped in ether. Elisabeth managed to sit up one final time, expressing her thanks and asking, *What is it that has happened to me?* before once again losing consciousness. When her companion Irma Sztáray opened the top part of her dress, she discovered the tiny stab wound, which was not bleeding. This was the first point at which she realised that Elisabeth had been mortally wounded. The ship turned around at once, and the dying Empress was taken back to her hotel room, the doctors being able to do nothing other than certify her death at twenty to three in the afternoon.

When Franz Joseph received the news, he said to his General Adjutant Count Paar *You have no idea how much I loved this woman* Elisabeth's death shook him deeply, and for the first time in decades he showed his mourning openly.

When Countess Sztáray returned from Geneva, she met the Emperor at the laying out of the body in the chapel at the Hofburg. He asked her to come to him at Schönbrunn the next day, since he had a pressing wish to speak to the person who had spent the last hours of the Empress with her. Irma Sztáray wrote about this final audience with the Emperor, at which, for the first time, he found it impossible to conceal his emotions: *My sad audience was heart-rending. When I handed to him the silver watch and the small fob chains of the Empress and the medal of the Holy Virgin she had worn over her heart at the hour of her death, there was great turbulence in the soul of the Emperor. Heavy tears rolled down his cheeks as I related all the details of the terrible tragedy …*

Audience of Countess Sztáray with Emperor Franz Joseph after the death of the Empress. Xylograph for *Das interessante Blatt* of 20 September 1898.

KATHARINA SCHRATT

Elisabeth herself had been responsible for introducing the celebrated Imperial Court Theatre actress Katharina Schratt to her husband and for encouraging their relationship. Katharina Schratt had been born in 1853 and was the daughter of a merchant from Baden near Vienna. She began her career at the City Theatre in Vienna, before accepting engagements in Berlin, St. Petersburg and

America. In 1879, she married the Hungarian Baron Nikolaus Kiss von Ittebe and had a son. She soon separated from her husband, however, although she did not seek a divorce. And returned to Vienna, this time to the Imperial Court Theatre.

Elisabeth acted as a real matchmaker for the two by arranging meetings, not an easy task given the nature of the court and its prevailing protocol. This mostly involved innocent visits on Miss Schratt's part to the reader to the Empress Ida Ferenczy in her official apartment in the Hofburg Palace, meetings which, by chance, the Emperor would also attend. Elisabeth knew that the Emperor would be in good hands with the cheerful and affectionate actress and used the situation to create a further piece of independence for herself. Katharina Schratt's humorous and comfortable ways soon meant that she was accepted and recognised as »a friend« both at court and in the family. She spent time with the Emperor and Empress on a regular basis, often being invited to family dinners. The tragic death of the Crown Prince seems to have been a particular catalyst which drew Franz Joseph and Katharina Schratt closely together. It was mainly from her that Franz Joseph sought consolation, writing on 5 February 1889: *Only a few lines today … to tell you that, in my unspeakable pain, you are much in my thoughts and I offer my innermost thanks to you. Your true friendship and your soothing and quiet sympathy were a great comfort to you during these last terrible days …* And a year later: … *if only I too could write so beautifully and lend the correct expression to my feelings, but I can only clothe my innermost thanks in the words which I can only repeat: that I am endlessly and terribly fond of you. How can I ever thank you enough for your goodness and comfort in the course of the sad year which has now come to an end? The difficult moments you have lived through with us are an insoluble bond for life, and let me express with confidence that our friendship will remain true and firm.*

Katharina Schratt in the role of »Lorle« in the play *Dorf und Stadt (»Village and Town«)*. Photograph, around 1880.

Franz Joseph soon fell into the fond habit of visiting »Madam« at seven o' clock in the morning at her villa in Hietzinger Gloriettegasse near Schönbrunn Palace Park to eat a second breakfast. Katharina Schratt always had a fresh ring cake and entertaining stories ready for the Emperor. They also often took a midday walk together in the Palace Park.

For Emperor's summer stays in Ischl, Katharina Schratt acquired the Villa Felicitas, in direct proximity to the Imperial villa. Here, she also served up the Emperor's favourite dishes, prominent guests such as Alexander Girardi or other actor or artist colleagues sometimes being present at the meetings. But she took care of the Emperor as well as entertaining him. Since he considered objects which could enhance his life as superfluous to requirements, she simply constantly made him gifts of useful items. These included a fan to make the hot, sticky days in his study more bearable, and a bedside rug. In their informal and frank correspondence, Franz Joseph often made fun of her predilection for unusual spa treatments, an area in which she obviously took after Elisabeth. When he learned that Katharina Schratt was undergoing a slimming cure in Karlsbad involving hay flower baths, he wrote: *I cannot quite understand the purpose of this new experiment and can only surmise that the smell of the hay must induce a condition bordering madness, in England at least so-called hay fever is a condition which can be treated by Dr Krafft-Ebbing* (the most prominent neurologist of the period, Ed.). *Until now, I had only been aware of the hay baths in Tyrol, where the farmers are buried in haystacks wearing paradisiacal costumes ... perhaps your passion for experimental medicine will inspire me to try this country cure for myself. The meadow next to the Felicitas would be ideally suited to the purpose. Incidentally, as with the Empress, I can only express to you too my joy and admiration of the power of nature which provides all these baths, waters, potions, powders and cold and hot treatments.*

Franz Joseph displayed an extreme level of generosity to Katharina Schratt. As well as a monthly allowance, she constantly

Emperor Franz Joseph in the »Incognitologe« of the Burgtheater. Drawing by Theo Zasche, around 1900.

received valuable gifts, mostly jewellery and gems, the Emperor also often paying off her considerable gambling debts. Although Katharina Schratt was not mentioned in the Emperor's will, the numerous pieces of jewellery he had given her over the years enabled her to continue to live a carefree life after his death in her palace on the Kärntnerring, bought for her by the Emperor.

Katharina Schratt was not, however, the only mistress of the Emperor's, and it is not fully certain that she was his mistress at all. Her correspondence, which cannot, however, be viewed as an ideal source in this respect, there is no mention of whether their friendship was more than merely platonic. It is true that there is talk of kisses in the letters, which are indicated as small lines, but quotations such as the Emperor hoped *to find her once again in bed*, have been taken out of context and do not represent proof of an intimate relationship, referring instead to what was known at the

Opposite page:
Franz Joseph on a walk in Ischl together with Katharina Schratt. Photograph, 1910.

Emperor Franz Joseph. Photograph, around 1910.

time as the »quiet week« (menstruation) which Katharina Schratt mostly spent in bed. She sometimes received visitors during this time, lying in bed in an elegant negligee, and Franz Joseph found these hours to be particularly cosy and intimate. Ketterl the valet also related *Mrs v. Schratt was not the Emperor's »friend«, she was a friend to the Emperor, the most loyal, best, most intelligent and most selfless friend he had.*

Franz Joseph had certainly had a number of mistresses before Katharina Schratt, including in the 1870's a seamstress in the laundry at the Hofburg Palace, a Miss Rosa Moskowitz, who withdrew into private life after three years' service at court. She received a court pension for life of

Anna Nahowski.
Phothograph,
around 1880.

three hundred guilders, later marrying Count Andreas Zichy.

Between 1875 and 1889, the Emperor had a steady relationship with Anna Nahowski. The two had met whilst walking in the Schönbrunn Palace Park, and the entries in Anna's diary show that they met on a regular basis over the course of many years in the early hours of the morning at her new villa in Maxingstraße next to the Palace Park, which her status as the Emperor's mistress now allowed her to afford. Anna was married for the second time to a civil servant from the Southern Railway Company and had five children, the last two being born during the period of her relationship with Franz Joseph. The Emperor's visits were always of short duration and probably confined to a single purpose. There were never any cosy hours spent chatting, as was the case later with Katharina Schratt.

Anna Nahowski did not receive costly presents or fond expressions of affection, and neither was the Emperor interested in her children, although two of them could theoretically been his. There is no conclusive proof as to whether Franz Joseph was really the father of Anna's daughter Helene, who went on to marry the composer Alban Berg, as is frequently maintained. There are certainly no indications in Anna's diaries to suggest this is true, and neither did Helen Berg ever make any public statement on the matter.

THE »OPAPA« – FRANZ JOSEPH AS A GRANDFATHER

Franz Joseph was touching in his role as grandfather. He had fourteen grandchildren, who enjoyed a far less distant relationship with him than his children. In particular, he spent a lot of time with the children of his daughter Marie Valerie at Wallsee Palace in Lower Austria, celebrating Easter and Christmas with them, but also paying short visits lasting a few days in between and enjoying the harmonious and happy family life. Above al, he loved the role of »Opapa«, as the children called him, spending hours playing with them, crawling with them across the floor, playing hide-and-seek or horsy and dutifully eating the imaginary dishes created in the doll's house kitchen.

Valerie wrote in her diary: *The children are his greatest friends, he even rolled on the floor to please Ella.* Valerie was on the verge of jealousy, having herself always wished for such a father, although this was a role Franz Joseph had been unable to play at the time.

Her children were not shy or overly respectful of their Imperial grandfather. They were jolly, ordering him around, and Valerie noticed that this was exactly what made things so much fun for him, noting in her diary: *It makes me so sad, and yet there is nothing I can do to alter things. Being together with Papa is like being forced to meet strangers. The children seem to sense this much less and are more intimate with him than I ever was.*

Franz Joseph on an Easter egg hunt with his seven grandchildren. In the background Marie Valerie and Franz Salvator. Lithograph, around 1910.

»The Imperial couple as happy grandparents.« Emperor Franz Joseph, next to him Empress Elisabeth and Archduchess Marie Valerie and her husband Franz Salvator. Lithograph, around 1895.

The influence of his mother had meant that Franz Joseph had neglected to establish a close relationship with his children, and this was something which he tried to make up for with his grandchildren. When they visited him in Vienna, they were even allowed to watch him at work in his study and play alongside him. He handed round envelopes from opened letters and coloured pencils, proudly keeping the drawings the children produced. As soon as they were old enough to eat on their own, they were even permitted to eat with him in his study. Franz Joseph, who had been silent and depressed in the presence of his daughters, especially after Elisabeth's death, now displayed the same measure of ease and joy in the company of his grandchildren, who offered him a few hours of late »family life«.

Right:
Franz Joseph at the playground with his grandchildren. Lithograph, around 1910.

Opposite page:
Franz Joseph with his grandchildren. Photograph, around 1895.

THE END OF AN ERA

Above:
»Kaiserlied«.
Palmin-collectible out of
the series 18, image 2.
Colour lithograph,
around 1900.

Opposite page:
Portrait of Emperor
Franz Joseph in uniform.
Photograph, around 1910.

GOTT erhalte unsern KAISER und beschütze unser LAND!

»God preserve our Emperor and protect our country!« Picture post-card, around 1910.

THE OLD EMPEROR

At the beginning of the 20th century, the political situation in the Balkans was reaching crisis point. Parallel to this, the militaristic system of the Habsburg Monarchy was showing signs that it was hopelessly out of date. Although Franz Joseph always pursued military affairs with the best of intentions, he was not a soldier. Although he always wore uniform and devoted a large proportion of his working day to military matters within his Empire, he became bogged down in details and bureaucracy. He failed to promote modern developments within the army and navy, the actions he did take even impeding this. The fatal element of the situation was that he had surrounded himself with military advisors and leading generals who themselves had little interest in change and knew that the Emperor only endorsed traditional outlooks and principles.

The heir to the throne: Archduke Franz Ferdinand in uniform. Portrait, around 1910.

Nobody wished to commit himself to presenting him with new, bold proposals or ideas. The reticence and complacency of his advisors, who also failed to inform him of innovations which had taken place in other armies, meant he lost sight of what constituted modern reform or technical progress.

After the tragic suicide of the Crown Prince, Franz Joseph's younger brother Karl Ludwig had become heir to the throne, after his death being succeeded by his eldest son Archduke Ferdinand, with whom Franz Joseph did not enjoy good relations. Franz Ferdinand was an arch-conservative, holding clerical and anti-Hungarian views. Only his insistence on marrying his true love, Sophie Countess Chotek, had accorded the Archduke any kind of public sympathy, and he remained unpopular. Although Sophie Chotek was of noble blood, she was not of equal rank with the Habsburgs, and this had set Franz Joseph strictly against the marriage. Only when Franz Ferdinand had foregone all rights to the throne for any children resulting from this morganatic marriage was Sophie elevated to the status of Princess of Hohenberg (becoming an Archduchess in 1909), which enabled the couple to marry in 1900.

Emperor Franz Joseph and Franz Ferdinand, during a manoeuvre in Veszprém. Photograph, 1908.

In political terms, the heir to the throne expressed vehement opposition to the aggressive and expansionist Balkans policy prevailing at court, putting his energies into the maintenance of peace. His public reputation as an advocate of an anti-Serbian policy, which drew the hatred of the anti-Habsburg southern Slavic nationalists upon him, was undeserved. During manoeuvres in Bosnia in 1914, which he personally took charge of despite warnings not to do so, he was shot dead together with his wife whilst travelling by car through the Bosnian capital of Sarajevo.

The murder of the heir to the throne led to the signing of an ultimatum, followed by a declaration of war on Serbia. The consequence of this was that Franz Joseph led his empire into a World war which was to cost nearly ten million lives and would finally bring about the collapse of his Empire. Franz Joseph did not wish this war, expressing the thought: *Those who want war have absolutely no idea what war is*, but his advisors insisted on a declaration of war, describing war as unavoidable and appealing to his sense of responsibility as Emperor. Just as he had done at the start of his reign, Franz Joseph acquiesced with the seemingly inevitable, thus sealing the end of the Monarchy.

His great nephew Karl was now named as his heir. Karl was the son of Archduke Otto, the younger brother of Franz Ferdinand. The »jaunty Archduke«,

Above:
Franz Ferdinand with his wife Sophie and children Ernst, Sophie and Maximilian. Photograph, around 1914.

Opposite and right:
Gavrilo Prinčip shoots dead the heir to the throne and his wife in Sarajevo on 28 June 1914. Retrospectively coloured newspaper wood engraving by Felix Schwormstädt.
The uniform tunic worn by Franz Ferdinand on the day of his assassination

as Otto had been known in Vienna, had mainly been conspicuous for a series of distasteful episodes. His son Karl, however, had been brought up by his strictly Catholic mother, had kept out of politics until his nomination as heir to the throne and was also largely unknown to the general population. In 1911, he had married Zita

Emperor Franz Joseph at the wedding of Archduke Carl Franz Joseph (later Emperor Karl I) to Princess Zita of Bourbon-Parma at Schwarzau am Steinfeld Palace, Lower Austria (to the left of Franz Joseph the mother of the bride Maria Antonia of Parma, in the foreground the six-year old Prince Gaetan). Photograph, 21 October 1911.

Emperor Franz Joseph with seven years old Archduke Carl Franz Joseph (later Emperor Karl I.,) in Cannes. Photograph by Archduchess Maria Josepha, 1894.

von Bourbon-Parma, and the couple lived in the Hetzendorf Palace near Schönbrunn, their eldest son Otto having been born in 1912. After the death of Franz Joseph, Karl was for two years the last Austrian Emperor, a position which was beyond him. His supreme command of the Imperial troops led to the long denied order to use poison gas on the Isonzo Front in northern Italy. The main burden on Karl's weak government at the side of his ambitious wife was, however, the untrue statements he made relating to the secret correspondence with his brother-in-law Sixtus of Bourbon-Parma, the so-called Sixtus Affair, which saw Karl initially denying having conducted secret peace negotiations with France behind the back of his German ally but later led to his being seriously compromised by the French Prime Minister Clemenceau when the latter published the letters. His withdrawal from government business on 11 November 1918 brought the Austrian Monarchy to an end. Karl died in exile on Madeira in 1922.

Emperor Franz Joseph and Otto von Habsburg, his grandson, son of Emperor Karl I. and Empress Zita. Photograph, 1914.

Franz Joseph on his desk.
Photograph, 1915.

In November 1913, Franz Joseph caught a chill after accompanying the Russian Grand Duke Nikolai Nikolaevic to the station in an open carriage in cold, stormy and rainy weather. When he returned, he felt ill and weak and, from that time on, laboured with a chronic bronchial infection, which finally turned into pneumonia in November 1916.

This was the first time Franz Joseph had been ill in his whole life since, as his put it, he had no wish ever to become ill and nor was he even allowed to. Despite a constant fever, the sixty-eight year old Emperor adhered doggedly to his usual daily routine and workload. Franz Joseph was not afraid of death, his fears centring on Monarchy which could die with him. On 21 November,

Franz Joseph received several morning visits, even feeling better than he had on the previous days. Towards midday, however, there was a rapid deterioration in his condition. He was forced to leave his desk and rested for a few hours in his comfortable armchair before once again having files brought to him at four o'clock, to which he added his final signature.

By now, his state of health was obviously worse and, at six o'clock, he was taken to his prie-dieu where he spent a longer time than usual in prayer before retiring to bed. He gave his valet Ketterl the instruction *I have not been able to complete my work, wake me tomorrow at 3:15 as usual.* Franz Joseph went to sleep, but woke a short time later, requesting something to drink, but his condition worsened. His breath became shorter and shorter. A doctor who had rushed to his bedside gave him a caffeine injection with the aim of stimulating the heart, but he was, by now, scarcely aware of what was happening.

At half past eight, Franz Joseph received the last rites in the presence of his family, adjutants and personal servants. Shortly afterwards, the Emperor stopped breathing, and, at five past nine, he was declared dead. Franz Joseph died at the age of eighty-six, having reigned for sixty-eight years. He had held the Monarchy together, and his death signified the end of an era.

Franz Joseph in uniform. Painting by Heinrich Wassmuth, 1915.

The burial of
Emperor Franz Joseph I:
the funeral procession on
the Stephansplatz square.
Photograph, 1916.

Emperor Franz Joseph
on his deathbed.
Drawing,
22 November 1916.

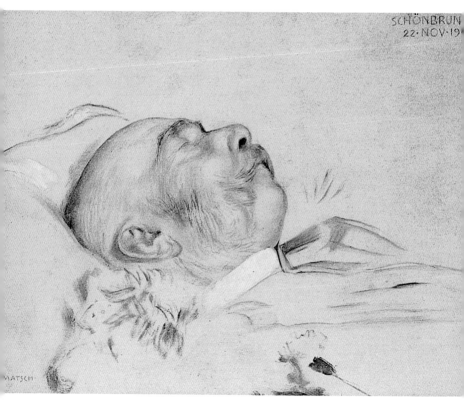

APPENDIX

Above:
Advertising stamp:
60th anniversery of
Emperor Franz Joseph's
reign. Colour lithograph
by Bertold Löffler,
printed by Chr. Reisser's
Söhne, 1908.

Opposite page:
[His Majesty]
Emperor Franz Josef I. –
1848–1908.
Wiener Werkstätte-
Postcard for the
60th anniversery of his
reign, No. 160, 1908.

SOURCES

Austrian State Archives, House, Court and State archive Vienna.
Varia aus der Kabinettsregistratur
Archives Wilhelm Weckbecker und Erggelet

BIBLIOGRAPHY

Cachée J./Gabriele Praschl-Bichler: *»Sie haben's gut, Sie können ins Kaffeehaus gehen!«. Kaiser Franz Joseph ganz privat.* Wien 1994

Conte Corti, Egon Caesar/Hans Sokol: *Franz Joseph. Im Abendglanz einer Epoche.* Wien 1990

Ernst, Otto: *Franz Joseph I. in seinen Briefen.* Wien 1924

Hamann, Brigitte: *Meine liebe gute Freundin. Die Briefe Kaiser Franz Josephs an Katharina Schratt.* Wien 1992

Holler, Gerd: *Sophie. Die heimliche Kaiserin.* Wien 1993

Kastner, Richard H.: *Glanz und Glorie. Die Wiener Hofburg unter Kaiser Franz Joseph.* Wien 2004

Ketterl, Eugen: *Der Alte Kaiser wie nur einer ihn sah.* Wien 1980

Kronprinz Rudolf/Vetschera. Berlin 1913

Nostitz-Rieneck, Georg: *Briefe Kaiser Franz Josephs an Kaiserin Elisabeth.* 2 Bd., Wien 1966

Praschl-Bichler, Gabriele: *Kaiserliche Kindheit. Aus dem aufgefundenen Tagebuch Erzherzog Carl Ludwigs, eines Bruders von Kaiser Franz Joseph.* Wien 1997

Saathen, Friedrich: *Anna Nahowski und Kaiser Franz Joseph.* Wien 1986

Schad, Martha und Horst: *Marie Valerie. Das Tagebuch der Lieblingstochter von Kaiserin Elisabeth von Österreich.* München 1998

Schneider, Josef: *Kaiser Franz Joseph I. und sein Hof.* Wien 1919

Schnürer, Franz: *Briefe Kaiser Franz Josephs I. an seine Mutter 1838–1872.* München 1930

Unterreiner, Katrin/Wohlfahrt Michael: *Habsburgs Kinder. Kindheit am Kaiserlichen Hof.* Katalog zur Ausstellung des Marchfelder Schlösservereins. Wien 2001

Unterreiner, Katrin: *Kronprinz Rudolf. »Ich bin andere Bahnen gegangen«.* Katalog zur Ausstellung der Schloß Schönbrunn Kultur- und Betriebsges.m.b.H. Wien 2000

Wallersee, Maria Freiin von: *Meine Vergangenheit. Wahrheit über Kaiser Franz Joseph/Schratt, Kaiserin Elisabeth/Andrássy*

Weissensteiner, Friedrich: *Lieber Rudolf. Briefe von Kaiser Franz Joseph und Elisabeth an ihren Sohn.* Wien 1991

1st edition

Cover design: Christian Brandstätter
Editing, producing and layout: Barbara Sternthal
Reproduction of the images: Pixelstorm, Vienna, a. o.
Printing and binding: DELO tiskarna, Ljubljana.

ISBN 3-902510-44-7

Christian Brandstätter Verlagsgesellschaft m.b.H. & Co. KG
A-1080 Vienna, Wickenburggasse 26
Telephone (+43-1) 512 15 43-0
Fax (+43-1) 512 15 43-231
E-Mail: info@cbv.at
www.cbv.at